ABOUT THE AUTHORS

Jeanette Edgar and Rachel Godwin met in 1996, when they
both worked for Rachel's father, John. Their joint business,
Alternative Meats, was launched in 2001 and is run from a
farm in Shropshire. Together they have built it into one of
the United Kingdom's most successful online suppliers
of British game and other unusual and exotic meats, and the
ups and downs of running a company together have only
strengthened their friendship. They were awarded the status
of Food Super Heroes by Rick Stein, and have appeared on
Ready Steady Cook, *Woman's Hour* and in the pages of food
magazines and most national newspapers.

THE EXOTIC MEAT
COOKBOOK

FROM ANTELOPE TO ZEBRA

JEANETTE EDGAR AND RACHEL GODWIN

PHOTOGRAPHS BY IAN GARLICK

FRIDAY
BOOKS

The Friday Project
An imprint of HarperCollins Publishers
77–85 Fulham Palace Road
Hammersmith, London W6 8JB

www.thefridayproject.co.uk
www.harpercollins.co.uk

First published by The Friday Project in 2009

1

A catalogue record for this book is available from the British Library

ISBN 978-1-905548-86-6

Project editor: Siobhán O'Connor
Art direction, design and illustrations: Simon Daley
Photography: Ian Garlick
Food styling: Sunil Vijayakar
Props styling: Simon Daley

Printed and bound in Hong Kong by Printing Express

Contents

Introduction

After five years of sailing around the world, Rachel, at the age of 25, decided that it was time to dry her feet, and returned to her father's ostrich farm in the Shropshire countryside to help with the family business. About the same time, I (Jeanette, 40-year-old mother of three) was recovering from a riding accident that left me with a broken back – and looking for a diversion to replace my lost career with horses – and so I applied for a job with Rachel and her father, John.

Rachel was to be hands-on, working with the birds on the farm, handling seven-foot tall ostriches, and I had a nice cosy job in the office making sales calls and marketing the products, or visiting restaurants and hotels to get them to try ostrich meat on their menus. It's been pretty much like that ever since!

I can still recall seeing Rachel walking into the office one morning, dishevelled and badly bruised because she had been unloading a trio of ostriches from a trailer and they all decided to vacate at the same time, without so much as an 'Excuse me'. There were cartoon-like foot marks all down the back of her shirt. The poor girl really should have been on danger money. On another occasion, we dispatched her to a farm in Gloucestershire to learn about incubating and rearing ostrich and emu chicks. It sounded quite exciting, driving around the fields in a pick-up with a circle cut out of the bed of the truck, then parking over the nest so that the eggs could be collected and a hasty exit made before an angry mummy and daddy came to see what was going on … but then, I was sitting safely in the office, listening to the story on the telephone.

Little did we know when we first met in 1996 that this was the start of our joint adventure in the world of alternative meats. Five years later, we were starting our own business together, the Alternative Meat Company Ltd, which was going to focus on all manner of different, exciting and innovative meats from all over the world, including our beloved Great Britain. A crushing blow was about to be delivered, however, that threw all our planning into turmoil. We decided to launch the company on 19 February 2001, but that very morning, as we were driving to the office in separate cars, we were both listening to a newsflash on the radio, announcing the first case of the foot-and-mouth epidemic in the United Kingdom.

There were tears that week as the full impact of the dreadful news began to hit home. We were sourcing ostrich meat from beef farmers who had diversified, and there was an immediate ban on the movement of cattle. In addition, our wild boar farmer in Cornwall could not transport his boar through the closed corridor of Devon, despite Cornwall having no cases declared within its borders.

We had begun to take birds of a feather from various local shoots, and spent many cold evenings plucking and preparing them for sale to local restaurants and hotels, but that – and the sale of local venison from parks and estates – dried up as the countryside closed down. We kept each other going somehow, going around the office singing songs such as 'Pick yourself up, dust yourself down and start all over again', which sounds crazy now, but desperate times called for desperate measures! Besides, we knew that there were people suffering much more than we were during that awful summer when so many farmers lost everything. We called a wonderful smokery in Yorkshire, Bleiker's, and persuaded the good people there to let us sell their smoked salmon and trout, and some of their other products, just to keep in contact with our restaurant trade.

But every cloud has a silver lining – we were awarded a rural recovery grant that enabled us to invest in our lovely website, and some nice new machinery for Rachel's cutting room. Shortly after this, we moved from Rachel's father's farm to a local farm shop. We had to orchestrate the transfer of our cosy portacabin over a ten-mile journey to its new home, and organised a crane to lift it over the farm shop into the adjacent field. Still, it was all good practice for our move in 2008 to our brand-new premises on the farm in Wem, where, I should report, we no longer have a portacabin for an office – we're all grown-up now.

Now we could begin to explore further afield, and we discovered that we were able to bring South African ostrich and other South African game into the United Kingdom, as well as kangaroo and crocodile. This was all to be done under the governing code of CITES (Convention on International Trade in Endangered Species of Wild Fauna and Flora), which ensures that such trade does not threaten the continued survival of any of the animal, bird or plant species concerned, or harm their ecosystem. Our mutual love of all things rural is always close to our hearts, and it was not long before we were investigating the wonderful diversity of meats that are produced by British farmers.

After becoming involved in marketing and selling RSPCA Freedom Food accredited rosé veal, we soon identified a need to wake up the farming communities and the general public to the opportunities on their doorstep – within every dairy industry, whether it is the production of cow's milk, goat's cheese or water buffalo mozzarella, there will be surplus male animals produced, and it is a passion of ours to educate people and encourage them to explore the options in available meat by-products.

Soon we discovered that there are other long-forgotten meats out there that were once the mainstay of the British diet, such as mutton, and we joined the Mutton Renaissance to help promote this wonderful meat back to the table. Thus was born our British Classics range, which also includes specialised breeds of cattle, such as Dexter and Aberdeen Angus, and pig breeds such as Gloucester Old Spot and Tamworth.

Looking back, we have enjoyed some tremendous adventures. We visited North Wales and were amazed to see a herd of buffalo grazing on the hillsides of the Halkyn Mountain; we drove down to Cornwall and were surrounded by about 20 little boarlets in a wood, followed by their parents, which was quite alarming. We arranged to come back through Buckinghamshire to collect 200 infertile ostrich eggs from a farmer, then spent the whole of the following week 'blowing' them with the help of an electric drill, a vacuum cleaner and two buckets. Believe it or not, an ostrich egg holds the equivalent of 25 hen eggs – that was quite a task! We went over to see Chestnut Meats, in Cheshire, who were going to supply us with fresh goat, and were 'accosted', for want of a better description, by an overamorous billy who had been brought in to meet his new wives that day ...!

Along the way we have tried many really unusual delicacies that we have not included in the book – besides the more obvious frogs' legs and edible snails, which you can find in any self-respecting French restaurant, we have fried locusts and fed them to my naughty teenage boys, who decided to run around the kitchen with the legs hanging out of their mouths to horrify us! (Needless to say, it didn't work. Locusts taste of a delicious mixture of peanut butter and bacon.) We were also invited to try rattlesnake for the first time on live television, which was a challenge to which we rose beautifully, I might add.

It was a very natural step for us to begin to cook and experiment with our meat products. After all, we could hardly sell something to a customer if we could not describe what it tasted like or how best to cook it. We attended many food exhibitions and shows to try to get the word out there, and were always called on to do cooking demonstrations with our unusual products. One of the highlights of our career so far was being asked in 2008 to speak to about 350 like-minded women at a WIRE (Women in Rural Enterprise) Conference. The subject was to be an 'inspirational' talk to ladies who were just setting out in their own businesses, or who might be in need of an injection of enthusiasm and laughter, but we were so proud to be asked because we had been in that same audience ourselves in 2001.

Our collection of recipes has grown alongside the variety of meats that have become available to us, which also seems to be growing at an amazing pace! We were asked by the Guinness Book of Records to attempt 'The Most Meats in a Sandwich', and managed to come up with 37. From British water buffalo, goat and rosé veal to crocodile and kangaroo, the range is as extensive as it is exciting. In fact, the title of the book says it all: from antelope to zebra!

If you enjoy eating meat, you are going to have fun. We hope that, after you have glanced through this book – with its wonderful photography and simple, fuss-free recipes – you will try something new, something innovative, something that you may never have tried before.

Jeanette Edgar and Rachel Godwin

Tips and techniques

This is the part of the book where we come clean and confess that we have produced this collection of recipes from a purely amateurish, passion-based lust for excellent-tasting food ... food that might surprise and intrigue you, definitely not for the faint-hearted, and something of a culinary adventure into the world of unusual exotic meats. We will be with you every step of the way – read on, and be fearless. And remember that your kitchen is a playground, not a schoolroom!

When using this cookbook, there are two golden rules to remember that will help you. First, all of the meats we feature are low in fat content, with little or no marbling. It is vital that you take this on board because it presents you with a golden rule: don't overcook. Meats with a low fat content are naturally lower in cholesterol, but you need to take care that they do not become tough and dry as a result of overcooking because this lack of fat means that they are not self-basting. Secondly, all the recipes we have included within these pages can be used with mainstream meats such as beef, pork, lamb or chicken. The recipes are simple and fuss-free (like us!), and it is only a small step to take to use kangaroo or crocodile instead of lamb or pork ... isn't it?

The simple things ...

To begin with, we believe that it's really important to have quality in the simple things – in the first instance, your essential cooking ingredients. We love freshly cracked black pepper. It is aromatic. It is peppery. Do not cheat. Buy some whole black peppercorns, and invest in a good-quality pepper mill – it's worth it. Likewise, sea salt. Lumpy and salty, but it has so much more flavour, and you can actually see it when you sprinkle it onto food, so you won't overuse it. Oil: use a good olive or vegetable oil and especially one with a high smoke point if you are searing meat. Please, it does matter, and it *will* add flavour to the finished result.

A workman is only as good as his tools …

If we had a penny for the times our fathers said this to us as we grew up … one was a master builder, the other a gentleman farmer, and both obviously relied heavily on the tools of their trade. So take their advice, and invest in a decent heavy-based frying pan or wok – or casserole dish or any vessel designed for the long haul. It will do the job properly for you, and it will last you for ever.

Next, a sharp knife – and a knife sharpener, preferably a steel, but there are other good options available if you don't know how to use one. Just make sure that the blade 'cuts', not 'rips', your meat. And use gadgets if you think you need them. No one will be giving you marks out of ten for chopping garlic – use a garlic press.

Dos and don'ts

Do assemble your ingredients when you choose your recipe, so that you don't have to send someone off to the shops halfway through preparing a dish. Tiresome, energy-draining and stops the creative flow …

Do check to see whether something requires marinating. We hate it when we are all set up to create a masterpiece, then everything has to go on hold for 24 hours!

Do prepare your kitchen before you begin – it's such a simple thing, but empty worktops and clean utensils make life so much easier.

Do try out your recipes on yourself and your loved ones before you entertain guests. Think how much more confident you will be when you *know* that ostrich fillet melts in the mouth or that camel makes the most fantastic stews ever.

Do, if pan-frying, wait until the oil is smoking before adding the meat – you will get a better result on the outside of the steak, which can be turned over to brown on the other side after 4–5 minutes. You can then reduce the heat to cook through.

Do present the end results of all your efforts with love, care and attention to detail.

Don't be mean with the alcohol – either when using it in the recipe or when having a sip while you enjoy your cooking experience.

Don't be afraid to step outside the parameters of a particular recipe – it's all a part of enjoying this collection. Mix and match different meats with different recipes.

The perils of overcooking

We will say it again: don't overcook. We know that we're harping on about this a little, but, believe us, it is the one golden rule on which hangs the success or failure of your safari into the exotic meats kitchen. Of course, there are some types of meat that benefit from long, slow cooking methods such as braising, casseroles and slow-roasting (mutton and goat are good examples of this). When it comes to barbecuing, grilling and pan-frying tender cuts of meat such as steaks and fillets, however, minimal cooking is key.

If in doubt, there is a simple touch test that you can apply using your fingers and thumb to work out to what stage your meat is cooked. First, lightly press together your index finger and thumb. With your other hand, feel the tension in your mount of Venus – the fleshy bit at the base of your thumb; there should be quite a bit of give. Now press together your middle finger and thumb, and compare the tension. Next, do the same with your ring finger and thumb; the tension will have increased one step further. Finally, press together your little finger and your thumb; the base of your thumb will be firm to the touch. The varying tensions that you feel are comparable with rare, medium-rare, medium and well-done steak, respectively, when pressed lightly in the pan with the tip of your index finger.

We recommend only ever cooking as far as medium-rare, even if you have the sort of guests who can't bear to see pink meat ... For the less faint-hearted, rare is just perfect. We once heard someone say that they liked their meat to walk off the plate if unsupervised – even better!

As we have already said, the important thing to remember is that the meats we have used in this book do not have any of the marbling or fat of everyday meats, which protects and lards them, and prevents them from drying out during the cooking process. Therefore, to achieve a succulent, tender exotic steak, you need to keep the cooking time to a minimum, or otherwise provide some larding such as wrapping the meat in bacon.

Springbok

Antelope

There are approximately 90 different species
of antelope. Four types of antelope meat are
featured in this chapter: blesbok, kudu, springbok
and wildebeest. All of these lovely creatures are
native to various woodland, scrubland and arid
grassland habitats in eastern and southern Africa.
The springbok, the smallest of the four, grazes
close to the ground and eats small sweet herbs of
the Karoo plains where it can be found, giving the
meat a unique herby flavour. You simply cannot
successfully domesticate antelope – they react
instinctively and extremely quickly to predators
and, being the second-fastest land mammal (the
cheetah, one of their predators, is the first), do
not take at all kindly to fencing! Interestingly, true
antelope have horns that are unbranched and are
never shed, unlike members of the deer family.

ORIGINS

Members of the Bovidae family,
native to Africa and Eurasia:
blesbok; lesser kudu and greater
kudu; springbok; black wildebeest
and blue wildebeest.

COMMON CUTS

Any guide to butchering venison
can be used as a rule of thumb.
Saddle (loin) and haunch are
used for steaks, medallions and
roasting joints; the remainder is
used for mince and sausages.

TASTES LIKE

Ranging from the gamy flavour of
blesbok and kudu, to the matured
beef richness of wildebeest and
the herby taste of springbok.

BEST WAYS TO COOK

Barbecued, grilled, pan-fried,
roasted, casseroles and stews.

SIGNATURE DISH

Springbok with blackcurrant
liqueur (see pages 28–9).

Blesbok

Kudu

Wildebeest

Moroccan-spiced kudu

Serves 2

6 fresh red chillies,
roughly chopped

10 garlic cloves, roughly
chopped

grated zest and juice
of 2 lemons

2 kudu steaks, about
200g (7oz) each

1 large bunch of fresh
coriander, stalks and
leaves separated

120ml (4fl oz) olive oil

100g (3^1/$_2$oz) instant couscous

1 teaspoon coriander seeds

1 teaspoon cumin seeds

100g (3^1/$_2$oz) green olives,
pitted

harissa paste, to serve
(optional)

Also good with
lamb

The heavy, aromatic flavours of coriander and cumin are very evocative of Moroccan-style cuisine, and usually associated with lamb or goat meat. Here, we have used kudu, with terrific results, as it has a flavour that can easily carry such strong spices. You can buy couscous already flavoured with lemon and coriander these days, but there is no substitute for the zingy taste from ripe lemons and fresh herbs.

1 Using a mortar and pestle, pound the chillies, garlic, coriander stalks and the juice of ½ lemon, gradually adding 60ml (2fl oz) of the olive oil, until a smooth paste forms. Alternatively, use a blender or food processor. This spicy paste flavours the kudu, which is strong enough to handle it.

2 Sandwich the kudu between 2 sheets of cling film, and pound with a meat mallet or the side of a rolling pin until evenly flattened and half its original thickness. Brush with the paste and a little more olive oil, and marinate for 10 minutes.

3 Prepare the couscous according to the packet instructions. Add the rest of the olive oil, the lemon zest and remaining juice, and the chopped coriander leaves to the couscous. Stir through, and fluff up the grains with a fork.

4 Dry-toast the coriander and cumin seeds in a medium-hot small frying pan for 1 minute. Roughly grind using a mortar and pestle. Add to the couscous along with the olives.

5 Heat a ridged cast-iron grill pan until smoking hot. Sear the kudu for 2–3 minutes on each side. Remove to a warm plate, and leave to rest for a minute before slicing thickly. Mound the couscous on a large plate, top with the sliced kudu and serve with roasted vegetables such as red and green peppers and aubergines, and a drizzle of harissa (if using).

Thai-style dynamite chilli kudu

Serves 4

2 shallots, chopped

2.5cm (1in) piece of fresh root ginger, finely chopped

2 garlic cloves, roughly chopped

2 fresh red bird's-eye chillies, deseeded and finely chopped

2 tablespoons groundnut oil

700g (1½lb) kudu steak, finely sliced

100ml (3½fl oz) whisky

a few green peppercorns

2 or 3 kaffir lime leaves, torn

110g (4oz) green beans, cut into 2.5cm (1in) lengths

1 tablespoon fish sauce such as nam pla

2 teaspoons rice vinegar or distilled white vinegar

1 teaspoon demerara sugar

small handful of fresh basil leaves, to garnish

Also good with
pork fillet

Not for the faint-hearted. A very good family friend of ours (hello, Nic) returned with this recipe after extensive travel in Thailand. We think that she deserves a medal of bravery for trialling this dish on her unsuspecting family. The lovely bright green of the basil complements the rich, dark kudu, and a bed of plain fragrant rice is a perfect accompaniment. We also suggest having long, cool drinks at hand!

1 Using a mortar and pestle, crush together the shallots, ginger, garlic and bird's-eye chillies to a smooth paste.

2 Heat the oil in a frying pan or wok over quite a high heat, and stir-fry the kudu for about 2 minutes until sealed. Gently warm the whisky in a small high-sided pan, and pour over the kudu. Turn off the heat, then at the edge of the pan or wok carefully light the whisky; once the flames have died down, return to the heat, and stir in the hot shallot and chilli paste. Stir-fry for another minute.

3 Add the peppercorns, lime leaves and green beans. Stir-fry over a high heat for about 5 minutes. The vegetables should still be crisp and brightly coloured.

4 Add the fish sauce, vinegar and sugar, and toss through well. Serve immediately, garnished with some basil leaves, on a bed of Thai fragrant rice (or basmati works well here too).

Kudu and bean stew with chorizo

Serves 2

1–2 tablespoons olive oil

1 onion, finely chopped

1 garlic clove, crushed to a paste with a little sea salt

200g (7oz) Spanish soft or semi-cured chorizo, peeled and chopped

a splash of sherry

1 fresh red bird's-eye chilli, chopped

pinch of ground paprika

pinch of cocoa powder

250g (9oz) canned butterbeans, rinsed and drained

3 ripe tomatoes, chopped

sprig of fresh rosemary, leaves picked and chopped

100ml (3¹/₂fl oz) beef stock

2 kudu fillets, about 175g (6oz) each

knob of butter

sea salt and freshly ground black pepper

handful of fresh flat-leaf parsley leaves, chopped, to garnish

Also good with
venison

We've used chorizo and chocolate elsewhere in this collection (chorizo with camel on page 45, and chocolate with blesbok on page 22 and with zebra on page 170), but here's an opportunity to use them together! The unusual thing about this recipe is that you make the stew and cook the meat separately; each then brings its own flavour to the final ensemble.

1 Heat 1 tablespoon olive oil in a pan over a low heat, and gently sweat the onion and garlic for about 5 minutes until soft. In the meantime, in a separate pan, fry the chorizo just until the oils are released. Add the cooked chorizo and a splash of sherry to the pan with the onion and garlic mixture, and stir in the chilli, paprika and cocoa powder until well mixed. Add the beans, tomatoes, rosemary and beef stock, and simmer for about 15 minutes.

2 Season the kudu well with salt and black pepper, and rub with a little extra oil. Heat a frying pan until very hot, and sear the kudu steaks on each side for 3 minutes. Reduce the heat, and add a knob of butter. Spoon the butter over the kudu to glaze it, and fry quickly, taking care to keep the steaks medium-rare, or medium at the very most.

3 To serve, divide some mashed sweet potatoes among 2 serving plates, and spoon over the stew. Top with the kudu fillets, and sprinkle with some parsley. Serve immediately.

Blesbok fillets with red pesto

Serves 4

4 blesbok fillet or haunch steaks, 150–175g (5–6oz) each

sea salt and freshly ground black pepper

For the red pesto

30g (1oz) fresh basil leaves

1 tablespoon pine nuts, lightly toasted, plus extra, to garnish

1 large garlic clove, finely chopped

50g (2oz) sun-dried tomatoes in oil, drained and finely chopped

30–60g (1–2oz) Parmesan cheese, freshly grated

150ml (5fl oz) extra virgin olive oil

Also good with
lamb fillet

Despite working full-time with all of these game meats, we never tire of experimenting with the various flavours and subtleties of the individual ones. Naturally, there are similarities that would make it difficult to differentiate with the naked eye between, say, a portion of blesbok fillet and kudu fillet, but there is a difference in taste, and it has been great fun finding a recipe to demonstrate this clearly. Somehow, red pesto does it for us with blesbok. You do not have to take our word for it – try it!

1 Preheat the oven to 190°–200°C/375°–400°F/Gas Mark 5–6.

2 To prepare the red pesto, put all the ingredients in a food processor or blender, and whizz until combined. Season with salt and black pepper, and transfer to a small bowl; set aside.

3 Now place the blesbok steaks on a chopping board, season with salt and black pepper, and spread with 2 tablespoons of the prepared pesto. Put the steaks on a foil-lined rack in a roasting tin, and cook for about 10 minutes in the hot oven.

4 Transfer the blesbok to a warm plate, lightly cover with foil and leave to rest for 2–3 minutes. Cut into slices, sprinkle with the extra pine nuts and any remaining pan juices, and serve with roasted or sautéed new potatoes and baby spinach leaves dressed with a little vinaigrette.

Blesbok medallions with port and Stilton

Serves 4

60g (2oz) butter
12 blesbok medallions, about 60g (2oz) each
1 glass of port
110g (4oz) Stilton cheese
125ml (4fl oz) double cream
sea salt and freshly ground black pepper

Also good with
beef fillet

A real winner in our eyes, this recipe has a simplicity that belies the stunning results and the sophisticated flavours that port and Stilton bring to the dish. We found that fairly small medallions, or discs, of blesbok were ample, so nothing more than 60g (2oz) each, with 3 per serving. The richness of the sauce added to the density of the meat will satisfy any red-blooded hungry guest – male or female.

1 Melt the butter in a large heavy frying pan until sizzling hot but not browned. Sear the medallions quickly, sealing them on both sides. Remove from the pan with a slotted spoon or fish slice, and set aside to keep warm.

2 Tip a glass of port into the pan, and deglaze, scraping up any bits from the bottom with a wooden spoon. Crumble the Stilton into the pan, stirring all the time, until it melts into the port, then stir in the double cream.

3 Return the medallions to the sauce, and cook gently for about 3 minutes. Season with salt and black pepper. Serve with game chips and broccoli – simple flavours to complement a really rich dish.

Blesbok and chocolate sauce

Serves 4

4 pieces of blesbok haunch or fillet, about 250g (9oz) each
60ml (2fl oz) sunflower oil
sea salt and freshly ground black pepper

For the marinade

1 x 75cl bottle of red wine such as cabernet sauvignon
8 juniper berries, crushed
12 black peppercorns, crushed
2 bay leaves
1 sprig of fresh thyme
1 strip of orange zest
1 carrot, diced
1 large onion, roughly chopped
4 garlic cloves, chopped
1 celery stick, chopped
sea salt

For the sauce

1 tablespoon tomato purée
1 tablespoon redcurrant jelly
40g (1¼oz) dark chocolate with at least 70% cocoa solids, grated

Also good with
venison or any other game meat

My son (Jeannie's) John has a horror of all things chocolate and was outraged at the suggestion of ruining a good steak with the revolting stuff. My daughter, on the other hand, was aghast that the steak might ruin the chocolate! Allow a couple of days to approach this as a work in progress, and use a dark bitter chocolate high in cocoa solids for the best results.

1 Bring the wine to the boil in a pan, and reduce by one-third; allow to cool. Put the meat in a large dish, and cover with the reduced wine and all the remaining marinade ingredients. Cover, and leave to marinate in the refrigerator for 24 hours.

2 Preheat the oven to 110°C/225°F/Gas Mark ¼. Drain the blesbok and the vegetables and seasonings over a bowl; reserve the marinade liquid. Pat dry the blesbok with kitchen paper. In a non-stick frying pan, heat the sunflower oil until smoking, and sear the blesbok on all sides for 8–10 minutes until a good deep brown. Transfer to a cast-iron casserole.

3 Using the oil remaining in the pan, lightly colour the vegetables and seasonings for about 5 minutes, then transfer the contents of the pan to the casserole with the blesbok.

4 To make the sauce, add the tomato purée to the non-stick pan and cook for 1–2 minutes. Add the reserved marinade liquid, and bring to the boil. Pour over the blesbok and vegetables in the casserole, and barely cover with 350–400ml (12–14fl oz) water. Bring to the boil for 1 minute, skim, then cover with a tight lid. Braise in the oven for 3½ hours.

5 Strain the juices into a large saucepan, and reduce over a high heat to 300ml (10fl oz). Reduce the heat until the sauce barely simmers, then add the redcurrant jelly. Check the seasoning, and whisk in the grated chocolate. Pour the sauce over the blesbok, and serve hot straight from the casserole.

Springbok Wellington

Serves 4

10g (¹/₄oz) dried
porcini mushrooms

6 shallots, chopped

150g (5oz) button chestnut
mushrooms, finely chopped

500g (1lb 2oz) springbok
loin fillet

30g (1oz) butter

2 tablespoons olive oil

2 thin plain pancakes

375g (12oz) pack ready-rolled
puff pastry

1 medium egg yolk

freshly ground black pepper

There are many ways of producing a successful Wellington,
but we always think that you have more control if you part-
roast the meat first, as here, especially when using lean game
meats, which require minimal cooking.

1 Preheat the oven to 220°C/425°F/Gas Mark 7. Put the porcini
in a small bowl, and pour over boiling water to cover. Leave to
soak for 20–30 minutes, then drain and finely chop.

2 Heat the butter and 1 tablespoon of the olive oil in a frying
pan. Add the shallots and porcini and chestnut mushrooms,
and sauté for 5–8 minutes. Set aside to cool.

3 Season the springbok fillet with salt and black pepper. Heat
the remaining 1 tablespoon oil in a heavy frying pan over a
high heat. Add the meat, and seal on all sides. Transfer to a
roasting tin and roast in the oven for 10 minutes. Leave to cool.

4 Place the duxelle (which is the shallot and mushroom
mixture you've just made) on top of the fillet, then wrap in
the pancakes. Unroll the pastry, then wrap around the fillet to
enclose it completely. Place the parcel seam-side down, and
decorate with the pastry trimmings. Transfer to a dampened
baking tray, and brush with the beaten egg yolk.

5 Bake the Wellington in the oven for 15–20 minutes until
golden and crisp. Allow to rest for 10 minutes before carving.

Roasted springbok with mango salad

Serves 4

500g (1lb 2oz) springbok loin or fillet

2 tablespoons olive oil

sea salt and freshly ground black pepper

For the mango salad

3 tablespoons caster sugar

4 tablespoons fish sauce such as nam pla

grated zest of 1 lime

juice of 2 limes

$1/4$ white or Chinese cabbage, finely shredded

3 carrots, shredded lengthways

3 long fresh red chillies, deseeded and finely sliced

5 spring onions, shredded

1 firm or green mango, peeled, stoned and cut into long strips

handful of roasted unsalted skinless peanuts, chopped

1 bunch of fresh basil, leaves picked

1 bunch of fresh coriander, leaves picked

1 bunch of fresh mint, leaves picked

Also good with
lamb or crocodile fillet

As you read through this collection, you will come to realise that the pairing of meat and fruit is a common theme and, of all the meats we talk about, springbok seems to call most naturally for fruit. Maybe it is connected with the light flowery taste that Karoo herbs impart to the meat, but somehow there is a marvellous synergy. The salad has a sweet–sour flavour, mixed as it is with sugar, lime and chillies, and we're sure that you'll think of many other meats to serve with it – crocodile is a definite option.

1 Preheat the oven to 200°C/400°F/Gas Mark 6. Rub the springbok all over with salt and black pepper.

2 Heat a ridged cast-iron grill pan until smoking hot. Add the springbok, and leave it to sizzle for a good 3 minutes or so on each side until blackened all over (about 10 minutes in all).

3 Sit the meat in a roasting tray, rub with olive oil, then roast in the oven for about 10 minutes. Remove to a plate, and leave to rest until cooled; carve into fine slices. The aim, as ever, is to keep the meat medium-rare.

4 To make the mango salad, whisk together the sugar, fish sauce, lime zest and juice in a small bowl. Put the other salad ingredients in a large serving bowl, and pour over the dressing. Toss together until everything is well coated, and serve with the springbok.

Springbok fajitas

Crossing the world in its influences, this dish somehow combines flavours and cooking styles beautifully.

Serves 2

grated zest and juice of 1 lime

1 garlic clove, finely crushed

2 fresh red chillies, deseeded and chopped, or 2 teaspoons chilli powder

2 springbok fillet steaks, about 175g (6oz) each

1 tablespoon olive oil

1 large onion, chopped

1 red pepper, deseeded and cut into strips

1 green pepper, deseeded and cut into strips

2 flour tortillas

To serve

guacamole

soured cream

fresh tomato salsa

grated Cheddar cheese

Also good with
skinless chicken fillet

1 Mix the lime with the garlic and chillies or chilli powder. Use to coat the springbok fillets, and leave to marinate in the refrigerator for at least an hour.

2 Heat the oil in a heavy frying pan until smoking hot, and sear the springbok on both sides for 8–10 minutes. Remove to a warm plate, and leave to rest for 5 minutes, before slicing into strips.

3 Add the onions and peppers to the same pan, and fry for a few minutes until soft and starting to caramelise. Return the springbok to the pan with any remaining marinade, and cook for a further 3 minutes or so.

4 Fold into the tortillas, and add the accompaniments to taste. Perfect healthy fast food.

Springbok with blackcurrant liqueur

Serves 4

750g (1½lb) boneless springbok loin or fillet

60g (2oz) butter, plus an extra knob for the sauce

1 wine glass of blackcurrant liqueur such as crème de cassis

125ml (4fl oz) strong game or beef stock

1 teaspoon tomato purée

freshly ground black pepper

Also good with
beef or venison

Another opportunity to bring together our favourite ingredients: meat, fruit and alcohol. It's a failsafe recipe as far as we are concerned. It is important, though, to make sure that, whatever meat you use (and we do love springbok in this recipe), you use the best – loin or fillet where possible. You can vary this recipe by using large whole 175g (6oz) steaks rather than medallions, but we chose medallions because they look great and cook quickly.

1 Cut the springbok into 10cm (4in) discs, or medallions, and beat lightly with a rolling pin to flatten them. In a large frying pan, fry the medallions gently in 60g (2oz) butter for 1 minute or so on each side.

2 Gently warm the blackcurrant liqueur in a small high-sided pan, and pour over the meat (take the frying pan off the heat first). Light carefully and, when the flames have died away once the alcohol has burned off, remove the medallions from the pan, put in a serving dish and keep warm.

3 Pour the game or beef stock into the liqueur in the pan, and let bubble for 2–3 minutes. Stir in the tomato purée, and season well with black pepper. If the sauce is too thick, add 2 tablespoons water and any accumulated juices from the meat. Whisk a small knob of butter into the sauce to make it rich and shiny. Pour over the springbok, and serve … beautiful.

Wildebeest with orange and apricots

Serves 4

450g (1lb) diced
wildebeest steak

1 teaspoon fennel seeds

1 teaspoon ground coriander

sprig of fresh thyme

1 garlic clove, finely chopped

2 small onions, finely chopped

2 carrots, chopped

2 celery sticks, chopped

50g (2oz) apricots, halved,
stoned and cut into thick slices

60ml (2fl oz) freshly squeezed
orange juice

100ml (3½fl oz) red wine
vinegar

2 tablespoons olive oil

2 tablespoons flour

600ml (1 pint) beef stock

175g (6oz) chestnut
mushrooms

sea salt and freshly ground
black pepper

Also good with
chicken

We hate it when we select a recipe, get all the ingredients together and plan the meal – only to find we can't actually cook it until the following day! So remember to start a day in advance to get the best from the marinade used here.

1 The day before, put the wildebeest in a large glass or ceramic bowl. Add the fennel seeds, coriander, thyme, garlic, onions, carrots, celery, apricots, orange juice, red wine and red wine vinegar. Season with salt and a good grinding of black pepper, and mix together. Cover with cling film, and leave to marinate in the refrigerator overnight.

2 The next day, preheat the oven to 180°–190°C/350°–375°F/Gas Mark 4–5. Take the wildebeest mixture out of the refrigerator, strain and reserve both the vegetables and the marinade.

3 Heat the oil in a medium flameproof casserole or ovenproof dish, and brown the meat with the vegetables in batches. Stir in the flour, reserved marinade and beef stock, and bring to the boil. Add the mushrooms, and stir through.

4 Transfer to the oven to cook for about 2 hours, stirring occasionally, or until the meat is tender. Delicious with mashed potatoes and curly kale.

Wildebeest rissoles with devil's dip

Serves 2

225g (8oz) wildebeest mince
1 garlic clove, crushed
2 tablespoons tomato ketchup
1 tablespoon capers, finely chopped
60g (2oz) dried breadcrumbs
1 egg, beaten
a little olive oil (if pan-frying)
sea salt and freshly ground black pepper

For the devil's dip
mayonnaise
tomato ketchup
a little sweet chilli sauce
dash of Tabasco sauce

Also good with
lamb mince

This is one of those really quick, simple supper dishes that is great for a mid-week surprise or to produce at the drop of a hat at lunchtime during the weekend. Wildebeest is just like any of the game meats in that it is a lean and dark red meat, and it binds together well to make these rissoles. You can either grill or fry the finished rissoles, but be careful not to overheat the oil or use too hot a grill, or you will burn the breadcrumb coating before the meat is cooked.

1 In a bowl, mix together the mince, garlic, tomato ketchup and capers until well combined. Season with salt and black pepper, and shape into 6 rissoles. Spread the breadcrumbs onto a plate, and dip each rissole into the beaten egg, then into the breadcrumbs until well coated. Chill until firm.

2 Preheat the grill until hot. Grill the rissoles for 8–10 minutes on each side. Alternatively, heat a little olive oil in a heavy frying pan, and pan-fry the rissoles instead.

3 To make the dip, mix together some mayonnaise and tomato ketchup to taste, adding a touch of sweet chilli sauce and a dash of Tabasco for a bit of a bite.

4 Serve as a snack with toasted pitta bread, the suggested tomato dip and salad, or as a main meal with potato wedges.

Antelope steak tartare

This is a last-minute dish – you need to act very quickly once you begin. I would recommend either mincing the meat using an old-fashioned meat mincer or an electric version, or chopping it very finely with a sharp knife – you do not want the antelope to be a mushy paste, which could easily happen if you mince it in a food processor.

1 Make a sort of pudding-shaped mound of the meat in the centre of the plate. Place the eggshell in the centre of the mound, with the yolk sitting inside, like a specially made serving bowl.

2 The piquant bits and pieces can be arranged artfully around the plate, then it is up to your guest to choose which of them to mix in, or not, to taste.

Serves 1

170g (6oz) kudu, blesbok or springbok fillet, very finely minced or chopped

1 egg yolk, kept in situ in the egg shell

1 small red onion, very finely chopped

handful of fresh flat-leaf parsley leaves, chopped

handful of pickled gherkins or cornichons

1 small jar or tin salted anchovy fillets in olive oil, drained

Dijon mustard

Worcestershire sauce

Tabasco sauce

sea salt and freshly ground black pepper

Also good with
beef fillet such as kobe

Asian water buffalo

American bison

Buffalo and bison

At last, an opportunity to set the record straight on these two very different beasts. When we refer to buffalo, we mean the domesticated Asian water buffalo (*Bubalus bubalis*) – a large bovine animal whose various breeds descend from one common ancestor, the endangered wild Asian water buffalo – not the African buffalo, which is an extremely dangerous and unpredictable creature. The bison, or American bison (*Bison bison*), is also bovine, and there are two subspecies, the plains bison and the wood bison (which is endangered). The plains bison is the one you might associate with Native American Indians and the once-great herds that roamed in a belt reaching all the way from Alaska to Mexico. The bison is also commonly but misleadingly called the American buffalo, hence the old song. There is also a species of European bison (*Bison bonasus*), or wisent, just to add to the confusion.

ORIGINS

The Asian water buffalo is reared extensively as livestock across Asia, North Africa, Europe and South America. The American bison, North America's largest land mammal, was hunted close to extinction, but is rebounding. It is found in the wild, but is also raised as livestock.

COMMON CUTS

Fillet, rump, sirloin and rib-eye are the best cuts; the remainder require braising or roasting, or mincing into sausages and burgers; both meats are very lean and much lower in calories and cholesterol than beef or chicken.

TASTES LIKE

Beef; bison tastes a little like liver when pan-fried.

BEST WAYS TO COOK

Barbecued or char-grilled (various cuts of both species), pan-fried, braised, slow-roasted.

SIGNATURE DISH

Bison steaks with Jack Daniel's sauce (see pages 34–5).

Bison steaks with Jack Daniel's sauce

Serves 6

6 boneless bison steaks,
about 300g (10oz) each

2 tablespoons butter or
olive oil

sea salt and freshly ground
black pepper

For the Jack Daniel's sauce

60g (2oz) shallots, very finely
chopped

60g (2oz) mushrooms, sliced

4 tablespoons unsalted butter

500ml (16fl oz) beef stock

175ml (6fl oz) dry white wine

2 tablespoons green
peppercorns, lightly crushed

125ml (4fl oz) Jack Daniel's,
plus 75ml (2¹/₂fl oz) extra

125ml (4fl oz) double
cream (optional)

a little freshly squeezed
lemon juice

Also good with
beef fillet

When making the sauce for this dish, pour a smidgen of Jack Daniel's into a small glass, and knock it back in one, smacking the lips appreciatively. This is a small gesture to Jack, to thank him for his contribution to the recipe. Also, a side salad of beefsteak tomatoes sliced through with red onion works perfectly with this dish.

1 Season the bison steaks with salt and black pepper, and leave to rest on a board for 1 hour at room temperature.

2 To make the sauce, sauté the shallots and mushrooms in 2 tablespoons of the butter over a medium heat for a few minutes until golden brown. Add the stock, the 125ml (4fl oz) Jack Daniel's and 1 tablespoon of the green peppercorns, and gently simmer until reduced by half. Pour in the cream, and continue to reduce until it has the consistency of a light sauce. Whisk in the remaining butter, little by little, then add the remaining peppercorns, the extra Jack Daniel's and a squeeze of lemon juice to taste. Remove from the heat, and set aside to keep warm.

3 Sear the bison steaks in butter or olive oil until medium-rare, 2–3 minutes per side. Transfer to warm serving plates, pour over the delicious sauce and serve with a tomato and red onion salad and some chunky chips.

Buffalo stroganoff

Serves 4

75g (3oz) butter
1 onion, finely sliced
150g (5oz) white mushrooms, finely sliced
2 tablespoons tomato purée
1$\frac{1}{2}$ teaspoons Dijon mustard
$\frac{1}{2}$ teaspoon paprika
110ml (4fl oz) beef stock
500g (1lb 2oz) buffalo fillet, cut into strips
150ml (5fl oz) brandy
200ml (7fl oz) soured cream
2 tablespoons roughly chopped flat-leaf parsley
sea salt and freshly ground black pepper

Also good with
strips of pork or beef fillet

Sautéing onions should be the start of every recipe. What a wonderful smell. This dish is much easier to make if you use 2 frying pans – unless you have access to a griddle for cooking the steak. Do try to keep the buffalo medium-rare to retain its tenderness and succulence.

1 Melt half of the butter in a frying pan over a medium heat. When it is foaming, add the onion and sauté for 2–3 minutes until just soft but not coloured.

2 Add the mushrooms, and sauté for 1–2 minutes, then add the tomato purée, mustard and paprika, and cook for a further minute. Pour in the beef stock, and bring to the boil. Reduce the heat slightly, and simmer for 3–4 minutes.

3 Season the buffalo with salt and black pepper. Heat a separate frying pan or griddle, and add the remaining butter. When the butter is foaming, add the buffalo strips and fry for 2–3 minutes on each side until browned all over. Gently warm the brandy in a small high-sided saucepan, pour over the meat and carefully flambé in the pan.

4 Add the soured cream to the onion and mushroom mixture, and stir through. When the flames have subsided in the other pan, add the buffalo to the mushroom mixture, and cook for 1 minute. Season with salt and black pepper, sprinkle over the parsley and serve immediately.

Buffalo and ale pie

Serves 4–6

900g (2lb) diced buffalo steak

30g (1oz) flour, seasoned with sea salt and freshly ground black pepper

100g (3^1/$_2$oz) butter

2 onions, roughly chopped

2 garlic cloves, roughly chopped

2 carrots, roughly chopped

150g (5oz) button mushrooms

2 sprigs of fresh thyme

1 bay leaf

400ml (14fl oz) brown ale such as Newcastle Brown

500ml (16fl oz) beef stock

1 egg, beaten, for egg wash

300g (10oz) ready-prepared puff pastry (preferably made with butter)

Also good with
beef braising steak

Here, the traditional beef and ale pie is transformed into something rather special by using buffalo instead. The ale lends richness to the gravy both in colour and flavour.

1 Dip the buffalo cubes into the seasoned flour, gently shaking off any excess. Place a large lidded pan or flameproof casserole over a medium heat. Melt half of the butter in the pan, and add the meat. Sear all over for 8–10 minutes until well browned.

2 Add the vegetables and herbs, then pour in the ale and stock. Bring to a simmer, then cover with a lid, reduce the heat slightly and gently simmer on the stove for 1½ hours.

3 Preheat the oven to 220°C/425°F/Gas Mark 7.

4 At the end of the meat's cooking time, season the stew with salt and black pepper, add the remaining butter and tip into an ovenproof serving or pie dish. Brush the edge of the dish with a little of the beaten egg.

5 Roll out the pastry on a lightly floured work surface until about the thickness of two £1 coins and large enough to cover the dish. Cut out a long strip of pastry about 2.5 cm (1 in) wide. Lay the strip of pastry around the edge of the dish to make a collar, overlapping the ends slightly and pressing down lightly. Brush with a little more of the egg wash, then lift the rest of the pastry over the pie filling to make a lid. Trim away any excess with a sharp knife, and gently press together the edges to seal. Cut 2 slits in the top to allow steam to escape.

6 Cut any leftover pastry into leaves, and arrange on top as decoration, using the egg wash as a 'glue'. Brush the pastry top thoroughly with the remaining egg wash, and sit the pie dish on a baking tray. Bake in the oven for 20–30 minutes until the pastry is puffed and golden. Serve hot.

Buffalo burritos

Serves 4

a little olive or vegetable oil

1 garlic clove, finely chopped

450g (1lb) buffalo mince

1 teaspoon ground cumin

1 teaspoon chilli powder

1 teaspoon dried oregano, crumbled

¼ teaspoon salt

125g (4½oz) refried beans

45g (1½oz) cold cooked brown rice

60g (2oz) Cheddar cheese, grated

To serve

4 large soft flour tortillas

salsa, soured cream, lettuce and freshly chopped or sun-dried tomatoes

lime wedges or halves

Quick, delicious and fun to eat, these burritos are ready in an instant, and it's definitely a talking point to use buffalo mince for the filling. It's also a healthy option, but we can't guarantee that your guest will know when to stop!

1 Wrap the stacked tortillas in a clean damp tea towel, put in a roasting tin or ovenproof dish and cover tightly with a lid or foil. Place in a low oven (130°C/250°F/Gas Mark ½) to warm through for about 15 minutes while you prepare the filling.

2 Pour some oil into a heavy frying pan over a medium heat. Add the garlic, and sauté for 30 seconds or so until white and opaque. Add the buffalo mince, and sprinkle over the cumin, chilli powder, oregano and salt. Sauté, stirring frequently to break up the mince, for about 15 minutes or until the meat is no longer pink and any juices have cooked away.

3 Combine the beans and rice in a saucepan, and warm through over a low heat.

4 Place a warm tortilla on a plate, keeping the other tortillas covered. Dollop a quarter each of the bean mixture and meat on the flat tortilla, leaving about 5cm (2in) at the bottom of the tortilla so that it can be rolled up.

5 Now for the pretty bit: add a portion of the cheese, some salsa, soured cream, lettuce or anything else that sounds good. Freshly chopped tomatoes or even sun-dried tomatoes are a lovely touch.

6 The clever bit is to fold your burrito correctly – you should fold up the bottom and roll the sides around the filling to avoid losing the contents! Make up the rest of the tortillas in the same way, and serve immediately with lime wedges or halves for squeezing over.

Oven-roasted buffalo meatballs

Serves 4

675g (1¹/₂lb) buffalo mince

1 onion, very finely chopped or grated

1 teaspoon dried mixed herbs

1 egg

225g (8oz) cranberry jelly

2 tablespoons horseradish sauce

1 tablespoon Worcestershire sauce

1 garlic clove, crushed

2 tablespoons clear honey

1 teaspoon paprika

1 tablespoon freshly squeezed lemon juice

chopped flat-leaf parsley leaves, to garnish

Also good with
a mix of pork and beef mince

Children will love helping you to make these meatballs – and also eating the finished results. The sweet piquancy of the sauce really works with buffalo, which has a slightly stronger flavour than beef.

1 Preheat the oven to 180°C/350°F/Gas Mark 4, and lightly grease a large shallow ovenproof dish.

2 Put the buffalo mince, egg, onion, herbs and egg in a large bowl, and combine thoroughly (mixing with your hands is easier, if a little messy). Using lightly floured hands, form into bite-sized meatballs. Arrange in a single layer in the greased ovenproof dish, and cook in the oven for 30 minutes or until done.

3 Ten minutes before the end of the cooking time, mix together the cranberry, horseradish sauce, Worcestershire sauce, garlic, paprika, honey and lemon juice in a saucepan. Simmer over a low heat to allow the flavours to develop.

4 Once the meatballs are cooked, add them to the sauce, and heat through for 2–3 minutes. Skewer on cocktail sticks if you like, and serve hot garnished with chopped parsley.

Tournedos of bison with chilli sauce

Serves 4

4 bison tournedos, about 175g (6oz) each

4 egg whites

2 tablespoons light soy sauce

1 teaspoon honey

2 garlic cloves, minced

3 tablespoons olive oil

60g (2oz) butter, chilled and cut into cubes

For the chilli sauce

3 bacon rashers, sliced

1 onion, diced

1 red pepper, deseeded and cut into strips

1 green pepper, deseeded and cut into strips

1 teaspoon deseeded and minced jalapeño chilli

110g (4oz) portobello mushrooms, sliced

2 tablespoons chilli powder

$1/2$ teaspoon ground cumin

1 teaspoon plain flour

300ml (10fl oz) beef stock

300ml (10fl oz) red wine such as cabernet sauvignon

a small splash of dry sherry

pinch of cayenne pepper

sea salt and freshly ground black pepper

A marinade infuses bison with a gentle hint of garlic and a touch of the East. This meat is slightly gamier than beef, but very similar in texture, so it carries the chilli sauce well.

1 Pound the bison tournedos with a meat mallet or the side of a rolling pin until evenly flattened; lay in a ceramic or stainless-steel dish. In a small bowl, whisk the egg whites until soft peaks form. Fold in the soy sauce, honey and garlic. Spoon the mixture over the bison, coating all the pieces well. Cover, and leave to marinate in the refrigerator for 24 hours.

2 Remove the bison from the marinade, and heat the oil in a medium frying pan over a high heat. Add the tournedos, and sauté for 8–10 minutes on both sides until nicely browned. Do not overcook – the meat should be pink in the centre. Add the butter to the pan and, once melted, coat the steaks in it to give them a delicious nutty taste. Lift the bison out of the butter, and transfer to a warm plate; set aside.

3 Using the same pan, sauté the bacon in butter and bison drippings until the fat starts to run. Add the onion, peppers, chilli and mushrooms, and sauté until translucent. Sprinkle with the chilli powder, cumin and flour, and stir through well.

4 Add the stock, wine and a splash of sherry; bring to the boil. Reduce the heat, and simmer for a few minutes – do not allow to boil. Season with salt, black pepper and a pinch of cayenne.

5 When the sauce is ready, divide the bison tournedos among 4 warm plates, and ladle the chilli sauce over the top. Serve immediately with wild rice.

Camel

Our only experience of camel meat has come – and you may be surprised by this – from Australia. Here, the population of feral dromedary camels is thought to be increasing at a rate of 11 per cent per year and numbers well over a half a million. How did camels come to be running wild in Australia? Well, think mid 1800s before the advent of the train – which pack animal would you have chosen to cross those thousands of miles of outback? Camels can carry up to 600kg (1300lb), and their soft padded feet do not erode the soil, making them ideal candidates for the task. They were used in the construction of the overhead telegraph line, and to supply goods to Alice Springs, Aboriginal communities and cattle and sheep stations. By the 1920s, however, camels were being superseded by motor vehicles, and so were released into the wild.

ORIGINS
One hump or two? This is how we distinguish between the only two 'true' camels of the genus *Camelus*; the dromedary camel has one hump, the Bactrian two.

COMMON CUTS
The most tender part of the camel is the hindquarter, which contains the sirloin and fillet, topside, rump and knuckle; forequarter meat is usually used for casseroles and curries.

TASTES LIKE
Camel is a 'sweet' meat of the type that goes really well with fruit such as plums and prunes, like pork goes with apple and ostrich goes with raspberries.

BEST WAYS TO COOK
Grilled, pan-fried, casseroles, spicy stews and curries.

SIGNATURE DISH
Comfort casserole
(see pages 46–7).

Simple camel with allspice

Serves 4

12 camel rump steaks, about
175g (6oz) each

1–2 teaspoons ground allspice

grated zest and juice of
¹/₂ large lemon

2 tablespoons extra virgin
olive oil

sea salt and freshly ground
black pepper

Also good with
pork

Camel is, perhaps surprisingly, quite a sweet meat, and we
think that allspice enhances the flavour beautifully. You do
not need to have huge steaks, as camel is rich and dense. The
suggested portion size of 175g (6oz) will usually match even
the largest of appetites.

1 Put the steaks in a large bowl or glass dish, and season
with salt and black pepper. Sprinkle over the allspice, and add
the lemon zest and juice, and extra virgin olive oil. Mix well,
cover and leave to marinate in the refrigerator for 2 hours.

2 Heat the grill or barbecue until hot, and sear the steaks
for 4–6 minutes on each side. Transfer to a warm plate, and
leave to rest for 5 minutes.

3 Ideally, serve on a bed of couscous, in keeping with the
style of the dish.

Camel, chorizo and red wine

Serves 6

450–675g (1–1¹/₂lb) topside or camel rump, cut into 2.5cm (1in) cubes

2 tablespoons plain flour, seasoned with sea salt and freshly ground black pepper

2 tablespoons olive oil

110g (4oz) soft or semi-cured Spanish chorizo, peeled and cut into large chunks

1 red onion, finely chopped

2 garlic cloves, crushed

300ml (10fl oz) beef stock

a jolly good slosh of good red wine

1 x 410g (14oz) can black-eye beans or butterbeans, drained

1 small bunch of fresh flat-leaf parsley, chopped

Also good with
pork

We first tried this recipe a few years ago, when it was given to us by a chef who was going to live in Tuscany. The addition of chorizo was a revelation to us, and camel was the perfect partner. On our first attempt, the camel was falling apart after just an hour; the second time it took a further three-quarters of an hour to produce the same result. Hence you will perhaps have to make your own decisions on cooking time for this one.

1 If finishing the casserole in the oven, preheat the oven to 170°C/325°F/Gas Mark 3.

2 Toss the camel chunks in the seasoned flour, and heat the oil in a large non-stick frying pan over a medium heat. Cooking in batches, sauté the camel and chorizo, stirring around the pan, for 3–4 minutes until browned and the chorizo fat is starting to run. Transfer everything to a large flameproof casserole.

3 In the same frying pan, gently sweat the onion and garlic over a low heat for a few minutes until soft. Spoon into the casserole dish with the stock and wine.

4 Bring to the boil, reduce the heat slightly, cover and simmer gently for 1–1¾ hours, stirring occasionally. Alternatively, transfer to the oven and cook, covered, for the same length of time. Test for tenderness, and adjust the cooking time accordingly. About 10 minutes before the casserole is ready, add the beans and stir through.

5 Serve on a bed of fluffy rice, garnished with chopped parsley.

Comfort casserole

Serves 4

500g (1lb 2oz) camel steak

675g (1½lb) floury potatoes
(the sort you would use
for mash)

4 carrots

60g (2oz) butter

1 large onion, chopped

600ml (1 pint) vegetable stock

3 or 4 bay leaves

8 whole black peppercorns

3 tablespoons chopped
spring onions

sea salt and freshly ground
black pepper

Also good with
lamb

This recipe was originally given to me by my lovely mother, who would never have dreamed of cooking with anything other than pork, beef, lamb or chicken. Mum called it 'tatarash', which I thought was a word until I was sent to my snobby girls-only high school, and I gradually worked out that my Mum's Lancashire accent had turned potato hash into something entirely different! Sticking to my roots, but adding a pinch of my current lifestyle, I tried her recipe with camel. When it is braised or stewed slowly, you have to go a long way to find anything that beats its flavour and texture.

1 Cut the steak into nice big chunks, and prepare the potatoes and carrots by peeling and dicing them into big chunks too – roughly 4cm (1¾in) cubes.

2 You can do all of this on top of the stove, so start off with a nice big heavy saucepan. Melt the butter, and add the onion and meat. Gently sauté until the onions are soft but not coloured. Tip in the remaining ingredients except for the potatoes and carrots, and season with salt and black pepper. Bring to the boil, reduce the heat slightly and gently simmer for 1½–2 hours.

3 At this point, the potatoes and carrots can go in. The casserole needs to be simmered for another 30 minutes or so until the potatoes start to disintegrate. Serve hot.

Serving suggestion Mum used to serve this up with red cabbage and chunks of fresh, crusty bread – I see no reason why these two accompaniments cannot be served with camel.

Bizarre camel

Serves 6–8

2kg (4½lb) roasting joint of camel (use the topside or sirloin joint)
sea salt and freshly ground black pepper

For the stuffing
5 tablespoons olive oil
1 large aubergine, diced
200g (7oz) dates, such as Medjool, pitted and chopped
½ onion, chopped
1 garlic clove, crushed
1 teaspoon ground cinnamon
juice of ½ lemon
60g (2oz) pine nuts, toasted
12 fresh mint leaves, chopped

Also good with
lamb

Oops! We mean bazaar camel, with its tantalising flavours and aromas of North Africa and the Middle East. Although it does go slightly against the grain to be completely organised when cooking – sort of stops the creativity – in this case, it definitely works to have the stuffing already made.

1 Preheat the oven to 190°C/375°F/Gas Mark 5.

2 To make the stuffing, heat 3 tablespoons of the olive oil in a heavy frying pan over a medium heat, and fry the diced aubergine for 8–10 minutes until golden. Lift out of the pan with a slotted spoon, and add to a bowl with the dates.

3 Heat the remaining 2 tablespoons olive oil in the same pan, and gently sauté the onion for a few minutes until it is soft and golden. Add the garlic and cinnamon, and cook for another minute. Squeeze over the lemon juice, and tip the contents of the pan into the bowl. Stir through the pine nuts and mint.

4 Open out the camel joint, and season with salt and black pepper. If necessary, butterfly the joint to make it easier to roll (see below). Lay the stuffing on top, and roll up the joint again, securing it with kitchen string or skewers.

5 Roast in the oven for about 1¾ hours until tender. Serve with some Greek-style yogurt into which you have stirred a couple of cloves of chopped garlic and some grated cucumber, and a big bowl of couscous or warm mashed chickpeas. Very bazaar!

To butterfly meat Lay the meat flat, with a long side facing you. Using a sharp knife, slice horizontally along the centre of the meat, being careful not to cut all the way through. Press down with your hand to open out; the meat will be thinner and twice as wide. This is suitable for thick cuts of meat and fillets.

Devils on camels

Serves 4 as a
starter or canapé

10 streaky bacon rashers
10 plump dates, pitted
200g (7oz) camel fillet or
rump steaks

Also good with
lamb

A bit of a different, dare we say it, exotic, take on the old cocktail party stand-by of devils on horseback. But we have found that camel works amazingly well with fruit, being sweet-flavoured itself. These morsels can either be cooked outside on the barbie, or you can sit them under the grill – but keep your eye on them so that they do not burn, and turn them frequently to keep them moist. Yummy!

1 If using bamboo skewers, first soak them in cold water for at least 30 minutes, to prevent scorching.

2 Preheat the grill or barbecue until hot. Take each slice of bacon and stretch it out, wrapping it around a date. Cut the meat into cubes about the same size as the bacon-wrapped dates, then alternate on each skewer – date, meat, date, meat, etc. Be scrupulously fair about dividing them between the skewers, or fights may occur.

3 Grill or barbecue for about 10 minutes, turning frequently, until the bacon is starting to crisp and the camel is cooked through. Arrange on a serving plate, and serve immediately.

Curried camel skewers with mint yogurt dip

Serves 10 as a starter or canapé

450g (1lb) finely minced camel
2 garlic cloves, crushed
2 teaspoons ground cumin
2 teaspoons ground turmeric
1 tablespoon olive or sunflower oil
1 teaspoon ground allspice
sea salt and freshly ground black pepper

Mint yogurt dip

1 x 200g (7oz) tub thick Greek-style yogurt
4 tablespoons mint jelly

Also good with lamb

Warning! Prepare in advance, as you are required to marinate. Ideally, you will also have some fresh rosemary stalks handy because these can be used as 'skewers', imparting an extra dimension of flavour to the spicy grilled kebabs.

1 Put all the ingredients for the kebabs in a large bowl, and combine well. Cover with cling film, and leave to marinate in the refrigerator for at least 2 hours or preferably overnight.

2 To make the kebabs, mould the spiced camel mixture into 10–12 cylindrical sausage shapes about 10cm (4in) long around each rosemary stalk or soaked bamboo skewer. Cover each end of the rosemary with foil to prevent burning during cooking. Grill the skewers for 12–18 minutes, turning occasionally, until cooked through.

3 Meanwhile, prepare the dip. Mix together the yogurt and mint jelly, and transfer to a small bowl. Serve with the skewers as a dipping sauce.

Note If you are using rosemary stalks for skewers, strip them of most of their leaves – you will need 10–12 stalks about 15cm (6in) long. If using bamboo skewers, soak in cold water for at least 30 minutes before using, so that they don't scorch.

Crocodile

The word 'crocodile' is thought to come from the ancient Greek *crocodiilos*, meaning 'lizard'. These ancient creatures appeared on Earth more than 200 million years ago, surviving even when the dinosaurs perished. The very stuff of Captain Hook's nightmares, they can grow to huge proportions. The largest type of crocodile is the saltwater crocodile, and the daddy of them all was found in Australia in 1957, measuring around 9m (28ft) in length and weighing 1352kg (2980lb). There is a 7m (23ft) specimen alive and thrashing in a wildlife sanctuary in Orissa, India, who could be well on the way to beating Big Daddy, as these creatures can live for more than 80 years in captivity. Strangely, perhaps, their eggs are only the size of a goose egg, with the little fellas measuring just 20cm (8in) long when they hatch.

ORIGINS
Various species belonging to the Crocodylidae family; found throughout the tropics in Africa, Asia, the Americas and Australia in fresh- and saltwater habitats.

COMMON CUTS
Although both the legs and tail yield meat, we prefer to buy the tail, which we feel produces the highest-quality steak. It looks like monkfish or cod, but unlike fish is marbled with fat.

TASTES LIKE
No, not chicken. Perhaps it is the marbling that gives the crocodile its flavour, and crocodile steaks definitely taste like pork!

BEST WAYS TO COOK
Barbecued, grilled, pan-fried, roasted, braised.

SIGNATURE DISH
Blackened crocodile steaks (see page 62).

Coronation crocodile cocktail

Serves 1

85g (3oz) crocodile fillet, cut into strips
$1/2$ teaspoon curry powder
$1/2$ teaspoon salt
1 tablespoon olive oil
2 tablespoons Greek-style yogurt
juice of $1/2$ lemon

To serve
handful of shredded Iceberg lettuce
1 mini pitta bread, toasted and cut into strips
$1/2$ lemon, cut into wedges

Also good with
chicken fillet strips or goujons

We were so surprised when the producers of the BBC's *Ready Steady Cook* decided to use crocodile on the show – certainly not a mainstream meat! James Tanner and Lesley Waters came up with some really great ideas, however, and this is one of our favourites. Not only is it really simple, but it also looks really impressive – and it tastes divine.

1 In a bowl, mix together the crocodile fillet, curry powder and salt, shaking off any excess. Heat the oil in a frying pan over a high heat. Sauté the crocodile strips for 3–4 minutes until golden brown all over and cooked through. Remove from the pan, and drain on kitchen paper.

2 When the crocodile has cooled slightly, mix with the yogurt and lemon juice in a clean bowl.

3 To serve, line the bottom of a tall serving glass with the shredded Iceberg lettuce, and spoon over the crocodile mixture. Garnish with the pitta bread fingers and lemon wedges, and serve.

Crocodile with chickpeas

Serves 1

1 tablespoon olive oil

$^1/_2$ red onion, finely chopped

1 garlic clove, crushed

85g (3oz) crocodile fillet, cut into strips

85g (3oz) canned chickpeas, rinsed and drained

$^1/_2$ beefsteak tomato, deseeded and chopped

1 tablespoon tomato purée

2 tablespoons boiling water

large handful of fresh spinach leaves

sea salt and freshly ground black pepper

1 teaspoon sesame seeds, toasted, to garnish

Also good with
pork strips

Another of a trio of crocodile recipes from the BBC's *Ready Steady Cook*, here tomatoes, garlic and chickpeas are combined for the sauce's base. These are perfect with the crocodile meat because it can carry flavours in the way that chicken or pork does. It is important to sauté the strips until golden brown at the start, as this looks wonderful against the white of the meat, the brilliant red of the tomato and the fresh green of the spinach leaves.

1 Heat the oil in a heavy pan, and gently sweat the onion for about 5 minutes until soft but not coloured. Add the garlic, and cook for 30 seconds or so until the garlic turns white and opaque. Tip in the crocodile strips, and sauté for 2–3 minutes over a fairly high heat until the meat is golden brown all over.

2 Add the chickpeas, chopped tomato, tomato purée and boiling water to the pan, stirring well. Reduce the heat slightly, and simmer for 1–2 more minutes until the crocodile is cooked through, then add the spinach. Cook for 1–2 minutes until the spinach is just wilted, then season with salt and black pepper.

3 To serve, spoon the stew into a serving bowl, and garnish with the sesame seeds. Serve immediately.

Spicy crocodile stew

Serves 4

a little olive oil

2 red peppers, deseeded and cut into chunks

1 onion, sliced

1 fresh red chilli, deseeded and finely sliced

3 garlic cloves, finely sliced

4 crocodile fillets, about 200g (7oz) each, cut into bite-sized chunks

2 beefsteak tomatoes, roughly chopped

900ml (1$^{1}/_{2}$ pints) chicken stock

1 teaspoon pimentón dulce (sweet smoked paprika)

2 bay leaves

sea salt and freshly ground black pepper

handful of fresh flat-leaf parsley leaves, chopped

Also good with
chicken breasts or
wild boar loin

We struggled for a while to find the right combination of spices for crocodile, as it is easy to overpower the meat's flavour, but the slight smokiness of the paprika is ideal and gives this dish a real Spanish touch. We can imagine this recipe working really well as part of a tapas-style evening, alongside fried baby squid and olives.

1 Heat a splash of olive oil in a wok or large heavy frying pan over a high heat. Add the peppers, onion, chilli and garlic. Sauté for 4–5 minutes, then add the tomatoes and stock, and bring to a strong simmer.

2 Now add the pimentón and bay leaves, and cook gently for about 20 minutes. Finally add the crocodile, and let it simmer for another 20 minutes or until cooked.

3 Season with salt and black pepper, and garnish with chopped parsley – oh, and don't forget to remove those bay leaves.

Chilli crocodile goujons with hummus

Serves 1

For the hummus
100g (3¹/₂oz) canned chickpeas, rinsed and drained
1 tablespoon sesame seeds
juice of ¹/₂ lemon
1 garlic clove, crushed
2 tablespoons olive oil

For the goujons
1 tablespoon olive oil
85g (3oz) crocodile fillet, cut into strips
¹/₂ teaspoon dried red chilli flakes

To serve
handful of shredded Iceberg lettuce
1 lime, cut into wedges
tomato ketchup
2 white mini pitta breads, toasted and left whole or cut into bite-sized pieces

We loved this recipe, again from *Ready Steady Cook*, because it combines some very familiar flavours with the exotic, and the hummus and salad can be prepared in advance, leaving just the croc to be sizzled in the pan. With such organisation, you could produce a wonderful snack or starter for your guests, with apparently little effort in the kitchen and more time to chat and drink wine!

1 To make the hummus, put all of the hummus ingredients in a food processor, and blend until smooth. Set aside.

2 For the chilli crocodile goujons, heat the oil in a pan until smoking, and sauté the crocodile strips with the chilli flakes for 4–5 minutes until the crocodile is golden brown and cooked through. Crocodile does contain a certain amount of fat, which when crispy-fried is absolutely delicious and oddly like pork in taste.

3 To serve, pile the shredded Iceberg lettuce onto a plate, and arrange the crocodile goujons on top. Spoon the hummus onto the side or serve in a small bowl, and garnish with the lime wedges and a drizzle of tomato ketchup around the edge of the plate. Serve with the pitta bread.

Indian-spiced crocodile steak

Serves 4

4 crocodile steaks, 175–225g
(6–8oz) each

3 tablespoons olive oil

1 red onion, finely chopped

1 fresh red finger chilli,
deseeded and finely chopped

1 fresh green finger chilli,
deseeded and finely chopped

2 teaspoons curry powder

1 teaspoon ground cumin

2 teaspoons cayenne pepper

finely grated zest of 1 lemon

2 tablespoons freshly squeezed
lemon juice

sea salt

Also good with
lamb steaks

After just a little preparation for the marinade, we found the best way to sear the outside of these steaks is on the barbecue, although you can use an indoor grill if the weather proves inclement. The marinade caramelises once subjected to heat, and the crocodile does not take much cooking, so have both the rice and naan breads ready to serve once you've put the croc steaks on to grill.

1 Put the crocodile steaks into a shallow dish. Heat the oil in a pan over a low heat, add the onion and chillies, and sweat gently for about 6 minutes until soft but not coloured.

2 Sprinkle in the curry powder, cumin and cayenne, and cook for another 2–3 minutes until fragrant, stirring continuously.

3 Remove the pan from the heat, and stir in the lemon zest, lemon juice and a little salt. Allow to cool, then pour the mixture over the crocodile. Turn once, and leave to marinate in the refrigerator for 1 hour.

4 Heat a barbecue or charcoal grill until the coals are medium-hot and any flames have died away. Grill the steaks for about 10 minutes, turning and basting with the leftover marinade now and then, until they are nicely browned on the outside. Serve with basmati rice and warm naan bread.

Crocodile fillets with vermouth and fresh herbs

Serves 4

4 crocodile fillets, about 200g (7oz) each
1$^1/_2$ tablespoons freshly squeezed lime juice

For the herb sauce

30g (1oz) butter
2 spring onions
10g ($^1/_4$oz) fresh rosemary leaves
3 tablespoons dry vermouth
125ml (4fl oz) fish stock
60ml (2fl oz) double cream
sea salt and freshly ground black pepper

Also good with
guinea fowl supremes or chicken breasts

We loved the simplicity of this dish, and the spring onions and herbs make a refreshingly light sauce that really lets the flavour of the crocodile come through – and it is very pork-like! The lime juice continues the cooking process of the fillets, so don't omit this important step. Crocodile is similar to monkfish in its texture, so it should be opaque and white all the way through when cooked.

1 Season the crocodile fillets with salt and black pepper. Sear the fillets on a hot barbecue or in an unoiled ridged cast-iron grill pan or non-stick frying pan for about 2 minutes on each side. Remove to a plate, sprinkle with the lime juice and set aside to keep warm.

2 To make the herby sauce, melt the butter in the frying pan over a medium heat. Add the spring onions, and sauté for about 1 minute. Add the rosemary and vermouth, and reduce until almost dry. Now pour in the fish stock, bring to a simmer and reduce in volume by half. Remove from the heat, stir in the cream and reheat until just about at boiling point.

3 Strain the sauce to get a lovely smooth finish, and serve the crocodile fillets on a bed of colourful couscous with the sauce poured over the top.

Crocodile fillet steaks baked with potatoes and tarragon

Serves 2

2 red peppers, deseeded and cut into strips

1 red onion, sliced

extra virgin olive oil

2 crocodile fillet steaks, about 200g (7oz) each

300g (10oz) new potatoes, thinly sliced

handful of fresh tarragon or 1 teaspoon dried

sea salt and freshly ground black pepper

Also good with
chicken breast fillets

A question we are always asked is whether crocodile is fishy in its taste – to which the answer is no, but it is in its texture and look. We desperately avoid describing to the uninitiated that any of the exotic meats taste like chicken, but having said that we can't explain why tarragon does seem to complement both crocodile and the aforementioned type of poultry really well!

1 First, prepare the peppers and onion. Preheat the oven to 200°C/400°F/ Gas Mark 6. Spread out the peppers and onion over a baking tray, and drizzle with some oil. Roast in the oven for 8–10 minutes until they are nicely softened and starting to caramelise, but not blackening. Set aside.

2 Reduce the oven temperature to 180°C/350°F/Gas Mark 4.

3 Lay the sliced potatoes in a baking dish, drizzling with a little more oil. Season with salt and black pepper, and roast for 15 minutes.

4 Place the crocodile fillets on top of the potatoes, then scatter with the roasted peppers and onion, and sprinkle over the tarragon. Season again, slosh with a little more oil, cover (most important) and roast for a further 15 minutes. The crocodile should flake nicely when it is ready.

Serving suggestion This is lovely served with a side salad of peppery watercress and rocket leaves.

Blackened crocodile steaks

Serves 4

4 boneless crocodile steaks,
about 175g (6oz) each
3 tablespoons butter, melted
sprigs of fresh basil, to garnish

For the seasoning

1 teaspoon sea salt
1 tablespoon paprika
1 teaspoon cayenne pepper
1 teaspoon garlic powder
$1/2$ teaspoon freshly ground
black pepper
$1/2$ teaspoon ground white
pepper
$1/2$ teaspoon dried thyme
$1/2$ teaspoon dried oregano
$1/2$ teaspoon dried chives

Also good with
pork steaks

Although we usually like to use fresh herbs in our recipes, there is a place for the dried version – when mixed and used as a coating, they work wonderfully well. Try to get the pan really, really hot before adding the steaks; the coating on the outside of the steaks will sear nicely in the butter. Adding oil will prevent the butter from blackening the meat, so try to avoid using it if you can. A couple of fresh basil leaves as a garnish will enhance the colourful roasted vegetables and add to the final presentation.

1 Mix together all the seasonings in a small bowl, and pour onto a plate.

2 Brush the steaks with 2 tablespoons of the melted butter, then dip both sides of each steak into the seasoning mix, pressing them down slightly to coat well.

3 Heat a ridged cast-iron grill pan or heavy frying pan over a high heat for 5–7 minutes until piping hot; do not add oil. Sear the croc steaks in the pan for 2 minutes, then turn over, brush with the remaining 1 tablespoon melted butter and cook for a further 5–6 minutes. Remove to a warm plate, and leave to rest for 5 minutes before serving.

Serving suggestion Serve garnished with some fresh basil leaves, on a bed of roasted Mediterranean vegetables such as tomatoes, red peppers, aubergine, shallots and courgettes.

Common pheasant

Game birds

It may sound like a contradiction, but without the sport of shooting game birds we wouldn't have quite so many of them. Steeped in tradition, it was once a royal sport reserved for the aristocracy. Gamekeepers looked after purpose-reared ducks, pheasants and partridges, creating and improving their habitats and therefore the countryside. Since the Game Laws were relaxed in 1831, anyone can obtain a permit for shooting game birds, pigeons, rabbits and hares. 'Driven' game shooting, where beaters walk through woods and fields, takes place on large estates and is overseen by a gamekeeper. 'Rough shooting' involves syndicates of shooters who use dogs to put up birds as they walk through woodlands or across moors. Each member pays towards the birds and their habitat maintenance.

ORIGINS
Common pheasant (*Phasianus colchicus*) Native to Asia and widely introduced elsewhere.
Mallard (*Anas platyrhynchos*) Widely known wild duck species.
Grouse Group of birds in the Galliformes order found in temperate and subarctic regions of the northern hemisphere.
Partridge Members of the Phasianidae family; smaller than pheasant and larger than quail.
Quail Small, plump members of the Phasianidae family.
Guinea fowl Originally native to Africa; the helmeted guinea fowl is widely domesticated.

COMMON CUTS
Whole birds, breast fillets.

TASTES LIKE
Ranging from the mild gamy flavour of pheasant and quail to the rich gaminess of mallard.

BEST WAYS TO COOK
Roasted, pan-fried, casseroles.

SIGNATURE DISH
Partridge stuffed with chestnuts (see pages 72–3).

Mallard

Partridge

Grouse

Guinea fowl

Quail

Braised mallard with orange and lime sauce

Serves 4

2 oven-ready whole mallards, about 450g (1lb) each

3 tablespoons extra virgin olive oil

600ml (1 pint) chicken stock

12 whole cloves

1 fresh hot red chilli

125ml (4fl oz) strained freshly squeezed orange juice

2 tablespoons strained freshly squeezed lime juice

90g (3oz) finely chopped red pepper

sea salt and freshly ground black pepper

thinly sliced orange, to garnish

Also good with
domestic (Barbary) duck

Wild ducks, or mallards, are not as plump as domestic ducks and have a much more varied diet – they are therefore not as fatty. Any excess fat there is will be removed during the initial process of this recipe, with a further skimming of the cooking juices ensuring that the sauce is not at all greasy.

1 Preheat the oven to 180°C/350°F/Gas Mark 4.

2 Pat the duck completely dry inside and out with kitchen paper. Cut off any loose neck skin, and truss the bird securely. Prick the surface around the thighs, back and lower part of the breast with a skewer or the point of a sharp knife.

3 In a large heavy casserole, heat the oil over a medium heat until shimmering. Add the ducks, and brown for 15 minutes or so until richly coloured on all sides. Transfer to a plate.

4 Discard any fat in the casserole, and pour in half the stock. Bring to a boil over a high heat, stirring and scraping with a wooden spoon. Stir through the cloves and chilli, then return the ducks and any accumulated juices to the casserole. Cover tightly, and braise in the middle of the oven for 1 hour. Remove the ducks to a warm plate, and skim off as much fat as possible from the cooking liquid. Discard the cloves and chilli.

5 Add the remaining stock to the casserole, and bring to a boil over a high heat. Mix in the orange juice, lime juice and red pepper, and season with salt. Return the ducks to the casserole once again, and baste with the simmering sauce. Cover tightly, and return to the oven for about 15 minutes. To test whether the duck is cooked, pierce the thigh of a bird – the juices should run clear. Transfer the ducks to a warm platter, and pour the sauce over the top. Garnish with orange slices.

Slow-roasted mallard

Serves 4

2 oven-ready whole wild
mallards, 400–500g (14oz–1lb
2oz) each

225g (8oz) fresh root ginger

2 long sticks of baby rhubarb

2 handfuls of chopped
fresh sage

1 whole head of garlic, cloves
separated, peeled and halved

2 red onions, finely sliced

2 wine glasses of marsala
or vin santo

150ml (5fl oz) vegetable,
chicken or duck stock

1 tablespoon olive oil

sea salt and freshly ground
black pepper

Also good with
turkey leg meat (the dark stuff!)

We usually find that half a mallard is a large enough portion
for one, and this is a fantastic recipe for roast duck, perfect for
a Sunday afternoon. The combination of ginger and rhubarb
is mouth-wateringly sharp against the rich duck.

1 Preheat the oven to 180°C/350°F/Gas Mark 4.

2 Season the ducks generously inside and out with salt and
black pepper. Coarsely grate half of the ginger and half of the
rhubarb. Mix together in a bowl with half of the sage and all of
the garlic and onions. Use to stuff the ducks. Sit the ducks in a
roasting tray, and roast in the oven for 1 hour. Reduce the oven
temperature to 150°C/300°F/Gas Mark 2, and roast for another
1½ hours until crisp and tender. While the duck is cooking,
you will need to drain off the fat perhaps three times (the fat
can be reserved, strained and refrigerated once cooled, then
used for roasting potatoes). The ducks are ready when the
skin is crispy and the legs can be easily loosened. Remove
to a warm plate, and leave to rest.

3 Drain off any remaining fat from the roasting tray. Pull
out all the stuffing, and tip out any juices from inside the
ducks onto the tray. Sit the roasting tray over a low heat, add
the marsala or vin santo, and loosen all the sticky goodness
from the bottom of the tray with a wooden spoon. This may
flame, so be careful of your eyebrows. Pour in the stock, and
reduce to a sauce consistency. Pass through a coarse sieve.

4 To finish, finely slice the remaining ginger, and sauté
in a little hot oil. As it begins to colour, add the remaining
rhubarb, finely sliced, and the remaining sage leaves, and
continue cooking until crisp. To serve, divide the ducks
evenly among 4 warm plates, sprinkle the ginger and rhubarb
mixture over the top, and drizzle with your tasty sauce.

Grouse with raisins

4 oven-ready whole grouse,
about 350g (12oz) each

175g (6oz) seedless Muscat or
other raisins

4 tablespoons sherry

250ml (8fl oz) crème fraîche
(or more if necessary)

60g (2oz) butter, cubed

sea salt and freshly ground
black pepper

Also good with
chicken breasts

The flavour of grouse has to be experienced to be appreciated –
I can only describe it as having such a pleasantly sweet gamy
taste as to be almost perfumed.

1 Preheat the oven to 180°C/350°F/Gas Mark 4. Put the raisins
and sherry in a small saucepan, bring to the boil, reduce the
heat slightly and simmer for 2 minutes until plump.

2 Meanwhile, put the crème fraîche and butter in a roasting
tin. Add a sprinkle of salt and a good grinding of black pepper.
Tip the raisins into the roasting tin (together with any liquid).

3 Season the grouse with salt and black pepper, sit in the
roasting tin and roast in the oven for 35–40 minutes, basting
the grouse frequently with the crème fraîche mixture. If the
mixture seems to be drying out, add a little water.

4 Serve hot on a bed of mashed sweet potato, and accompany
with fresh green vegetables such as French beans, tenderstem
broccoli and mangetout.

Casserole of grouse

Serves 4

4 tablespoons groundnut oil

4 oven-ready whole grouse, about 350g (12oz) each

12 shallots, peeled but left whole

4 celery sticks, thickly sliced

250g (9oz) button mushrooms, wiped clean

30g (1oz) plain flour

600ml (1 pint) chicken stock

3 sprigs of fresh thyme

1 sprig of fresh rosemary

2 tablespoons cognac

60ml (2fl oz) double cream

sea salt and freshly ground black pepper

Also good with
lamb shanks

This little bird is so highly prized, and no wonder, with its deliciously rich flavour and tiny size. The meat will be almost falling from the bone at the end of the cooking time, mouth-watering and astonishingly good. One bird per person is the order of the day – no more, no less.

1 Preheat the oven to 180°C/350°F/Gas Mark 4.

2 Heat the oil in a large flameproof casserole until very hot. Carefully add the grouse, 2 at a time, and brown on all sides for 10 minutes. Remove from the casserole, and set aside.

3 Add the shallots, celery and mushrooms to the casserole, and sauté for 5 minutes, stirring from time to time, until softened. Sprinkle the flour over the mixture, and cook, stirring, for 1–2 minutes.

4 Gradually blend in the stock, stirring constantly, then add the thyme and rosemary, and season with salt and black pepper. Simmer for 3–4 minutes. Return the grouse to the pan, mix well, then cover and cook in the oven for 1½ hours.

5 Just before serving, gently warm the cognac in a ladle or small high-sided pan, and carefully set alight. Add to the casserole together with the cream, and mix well. Serve hot.

Devilled quail

Serves 2

4 oven-ready whole quail
1 tablespoon groundnut oil
4 garlic cloves, crushed
1 teaspoon cayenne pepper
juice of $1/2$ lemon
2 tablespoons light soy sauce
$1/2$ teaspoon salt
4 teaspoons wholegrain
mustard

Also good with
pork chops

These are very tiny birds, so you will need 2 of each per person at least! They should become rather sticky and, as it is both fun and practical to pick the meat off the birds with your fingers, we recommend a finger bowl.

1 Preheat the oven to 220°C/425°F/Gas Mark 7.

2 In a small bowl, mix together the oil, garlic, cayenne, lemon juice, soy sauce, salt and mustard.

3 Sit the quail in a small roasting tin, and pour over the mixture so that the birds are soaked in it and some of it drizzles into the pan. Roast in the oven for 20–25 minutes, basting once. Serve with something very simple such as brown rice or freshly baked warm French bread.

Partridge stuffed with chestnuts

aServes 4

60g (2oz) butter

2 shallots, finely chopped

4 oven-ready whole partridge, about 350g (12oz) each

4 chicken livers (or use those reserved from the partridges), halved

450g (1lb) peeled chestnuts

150ml (5fl oz) whole milk

about 250ml (8fl oz) chicken stock

8 streaky bacon rashers

sea salt and freshly ground black pepper

Also good with
chicken

These flavours and textures are a marriage made in heaven – the slightly nutty sweetness of the chestnuts, the crunchy texture mixed with the smooth livers, the crispy bacon on top of plump, juicy partridge breasts. Roasted winter vegetables such as parsnips, celeriac and Jerusalem artichokes provide a beautiful complement to these birds.

1 Melt the butter in a heavy frying pan over a low heat. Add the shallots, and sweat gently for a few minutes until soft. Now add the livers to the pan, along with the chestnuts, and cook gently for about 5 minutes. Transfer the contents of the pan to a small bowl, and cover with the milk. Leave to stand for about 30 minutes.

2 Preheat the oven to 220°C/425°F/Gas Mark 7. Either by hand or using a food processor, mash the chestnut and liver mixture, but be careful not to purée it to a paste – leave it a little lumpy. Use to stuff each partridge, reserving a small amount of this stuffing to make the sauce. Truss the birds to prevent the stuffing leaking. Cover with the streaky bacon, put in a roasting tin and roast in the oven for about 20 minutes.

3 Remove the bacon, and return the partridge to the oven for a further 10 minutes until the breasts are golden brown. Put them on a warm plate, cover loosely with foil and leave to rest for 10 minutes. Sit the tin over a medium-high heat, and pour in a little stock and the reserved stuffing. Using a wooden spoon to scrape up any bits from the bottom of the tin, keep stirring and scraping until the sauce starts to bubble and reduce, adding a little more stock if needed. Season with salt and black pepper, and serve poured over the birds.

Tipsy pheasant fillets

Using our ready-prepared pheasant fillets (4 in a pack) makes this very simple, and will give 4 people a decent serving each. If you like, you can add chestnuts to the recipe, turning it into something festive and wintry.

Serves 4

4 pheasant breast fillets, about 110g (4oz) each

1 tablespoon olive oil

1 tablespoon butter

225g (8oz) baby onions or shallots

2 tablespoons flour

200ml (7fl oz) dry white wine

150ml (5fl oz) chicken stock

1 tablespoon redcurrant jelly

zest of 1 orange, cut into julienne

juice of 2 oranges

2 tablespoons brandy

1 bay leaf

sea salt and freshly ground black pepper

a few sprigs of watercress, to garnish

Also good with
turkey breast fillets

1 Preheat the oven to 180°C/350°F/Gas Mark 4.

2 Sprinkle the pheasant breasts with salt and pepper. Heat the oil and butter in a heavy frying pan, and fry the pieces for 7 minutes until browned all over. Transfer to a casserole.

3 Using the same pan, sauté the onions or shallots for a few minutes until lightly coloured, and arrange in the casserole with the pheasant fillets. If using chestnuts, now is the time to add them.

4 Stir the flour into the frying pan, and cook for 1 minute, adding the wine and stock gradually and scraping up any bits from the bottom with a wooden spoon. Stir in the redcurrant jelly, orange zest and juice, and brandy, and add the bay leaf. Pour over the pheasant, cover and cook for 50–60 minutes – check to see whether it is tender; if it is, stop cooking!

5 Discard the bay leaf, and serve garnished with a few sprigs of watercress. This is quite a rich dish, so it is best to stick to something simple as an accompaniment, such as brown rice or creamed potatoes.

Pheasant cacciatore

Serves 6

about 4 tablespoons olive oil

1 onion, finely chopped

2 garlic cloves, crushed

6 pheasant supremes (breasts with wing attached), skin on

2 x 400g (14oz) cans peeled whole plum tomatoes, chopped, or use fresh cherry tomatoes

4 tablespoons mascarpone cheese

handful of fresh basil leaves

sea salt and freshly ground black pepper

The name of this dish means 'pheasant, cooked hunter-style', and it is a simple and delicious way to produce pheasant for a family. The freshness of the tomatoes and basil makes a lovely light sauce that children will love.

1 Preheat the oven to 190°C/375°F/Gas Mark 5.

2 In a heavy frying pan, sweat the onion in about 3 tablespoons olive oil over a low heat for about 5 minutes until soft but not coloured. Add the garlic, and cook for about 30 seconds more until the garlic turns white and opaque.

3 Tip in the tomatoes, including any juices (if fresh, they will take a little while to break down). Season with sea salt and black pepper, and simmer gently until you have a thick, glossy sauce. Stir through the mascarpone, and tear in half of the fresh basil leaves. (Always tear your basil where possible; never cut. There is a distinct difference in the strength of flavour when the leaves are roughly torn.)

4 Now take the pheasant supremes, and fry them in a little olive oil for about 7 minutes until nicely golden. Transfer to a baking dish, and pour over the tomato sauce. Cook in the oven for up to 50 minutes until cooked through – the sauce helps to prevent the pheasant meat drying out.

5 Scatter over the rest of the basil leaves to garnish, and serve.

Lemon and thyme pheasant fillets

Serves 2

2 tablespoons olive oil
juice of 1–2 lemons
3 sprigs of fresh thyme
2 garlic cloves, crushed
4 large pheasant breast fillets,
about 110g (4oz) each,
butterflied (see page 48)

Also good with
pork tenderloin

We are using really light flavours on a gamy meat here, and the result is pleasantly light and flavoursome. Most unusual. Serving the fillets with a vegetable in a creamy or cheesy sauce counteracts the gamy, slightly dry flavour of the pheasant, and makes for a wonderful partnership.

1 In a small bowl, whisk together the oil, lemon juice, thyme and garlic to make a marinade. Lay the pheasant in a shallow glass or ceramic dish, pour over the marinade, and leave to marinate in the refrigerator for 1 hour.

2 Heat a ridged cast-iron grill pan or heavy frying pan over a high heat. Sear the fillets for about 8 minutes on each side (use a little of the marinade if cooking in a frying pan). Make sure that the fillets are cooked through and have browned nicely on the outside. Remove to a warm plate, and leave to rest for about 5 minutes.

3 Serve with leeks in béchamel, cauliflower and broccoli baked in a cheese sauce, or something similarly creamy.

Courgette-stuffed pheasant breast

Serves 4

4 large skinless pheasant breast fillets, about 110g (4oz) each

2 tablespoons butter

2 courgettes, shredded

3 slices white bread

1 egg white

1 tablespoon olive oil

300g (10oz) soft cheese such as mozzarella, grated

garlic salt

coarsely ground black pepper

dash of paprika

Also good with
skinless chicken breast fillets

The stuffing in this recipe is moist and mild, and as such works really well with the pheasant. The cheese should bubble and turn golden as it oozes out of the fillets, adding texture and colour to the meat.

1 Preheat the oven to 180°C/350°F/Gas Mark 4.

2 Melt the butter in a frying pan over a medium-high heat, and sauté the courgettes for several minutes until softened. Roughly tear the bread into pieces, and add to the courgette, along with the egg white, oil and cheese. Stir through well, and remove from the heat.

3 Season the pheasant breasts with the garlic salt, black pepper and paprika. Using a sharp knife, split them down the centre to create a pocket. Divide the stuffing evenly among the fillets, and push into each pocket and over the top of the fillet.

4 Place the fillets stuffing-side up in a heavy casserole, cover and bake in the oven for about 40 minutes until tender. Serve with mashed sweet potato and sugar snap peas.

Home-made pheasant burgers

Serves 4

500g (1lb 2oz) skinless pheasant breast fillets

1 small onion, finely chopped

3 medium courgettes, grated

splash of light soy sauce

1 teaspoon freshly grated root ginger

1 egg yolk

a little olive oil

sea salt and freshly ground black pepper

Also good with
chicken mince

This is an incredibly quick, simple but innovative way to serve pheasant. The combination of traditional game with a thoroughly modern method of presentation, i.e. the 'burger', provides an unexpected and tasty supper dish.

1 Mince the pheasant breasts, and mix together with the onion, courgettes, soy sauce and ginger in a bowl, adding the egg at the end. Season with salt and black pepper. Using lightly floured hands, divide the mixture into 4 balls, and press into burger shapes. Chill until firm.

2 Preheat the grill until hot. Line a grill pan with foil, and arrange your burgers on the grill rack, brushing lightly with a good olive oil. Grill for about 10 minutes until cooked through, turning 2 or 3 times during cooking.

3 Serve with a fresh tomato and onion relish and some crisp salad leaves, or sandwich between a bun with sliced tomato, onion and lettuce.

Roast pheasant with apricots and dates

Serves 4

90g (3oz) dried apricots

125ml (4fl oz) dry white wine

60ml (2fl oz) Grand Marnier liqueur

60ml (2fl oz) freshly squeezed lime juice

2 tablespoons sugar

2 teaspoons dried thyme, crumbled

2 bay leaves

a little vegetable oil

90g (3oz) pitted dates, chopped

2 oven-ready whole pheasants, 1.1–1.35kg (2¹/₂-3lb) in total

freshly ground black pepper

a few sprigs of fresh thyme, to garnish

Also good with pork chops

You have to love the combination of dates and apricots – pure genius! They make the sauce very sticky and slightly sweet, but it is unforgettable combined with the pheasant meat. Resting the birds is quite an important stage, as it greatly helps when carving the birds at the table.

1 Preheat the oven to 200°C/400°F/Gas Mark 6.

2 In a small heatproof bowl, cover the apricots with boiling water, and leave to soak for 10 minutes. Drain the apricots, and cut into quarters. In a small saucepan, gently simmer the wine, liqueur, lime juice, sugar, dried thyme and bay leaves for 5 minutes.

3 Brush the pheasants with a little oil, and arrange breast-side down in a roasting tin. Roast the pheasants in the oven for 20 minutes, then discard any fat in the roasting tin. Turn the pheasants over, and add the chopped apricots, wine mixture and dates to the pan. Return to the oven to roast for a further 25 minutes, adding about 125ml (4fl oz) water if all the liquid evaporates. Leave the pheasants to rest in a warm place for 10 minutes before serving.

4 Transfer the birds to a cutting board, and cut each one in half – kitchen scissors are good for this. Serve with the apricot and date sauce spooned over and garnished with a few sprigs of fresh thyme.

Pheasant with cream and apples

Serves 2

30g (1oz) butter
1 tablespoon olive oil
1 oven-ready plump young whole pheasant
1 onion, finely chopped
2 medium cooking apples such as Bramley
175ml (6fl oz) cider
125ml (4fl oz) double cream
sea salt and freshly ground black pepper

Also good with
guinea fowl supremes

Our customers have often shared their family recipes with us, and one of our favourites, Mrs Bradley, handwrote this and sent it to us about 5 years ago, having cooked it for her husband for many years. If you don't have any cider on hand, use a dry white wine instead.

1 Heat the butter and oil together in a flameproof casserole or heavy pan over a medium heat. Season the pheasant with salt and black pepper, and brown in the pan, turning the bird regularly so that it is evenly coloured. Add the onion, and sauté for about 5 minutes until soft.

2 Meanwhile, peel and core the apples. Cut into chunky slices, and stir them into the casserole. Add the cider, and gently cook over a low heat for about 1 hour, turning the bird onto the other side about halfway through the cooking time.

3 When the bird is cooked, remove to a serving dish and keep warm. Simmer the liquid until it has reduced, then reduce the heat and stir in the cream. Season with salt and black pepper, and heat gently, stirring, then pour over the bird and serve.

Pheasant fillets with glazed butternut squash

Serves 4

500g (1lb 2oz) butternut squash, peeled, deseeded and cut into 4cm (³/₄in) chunks

60g (2oz) butter

1 tablespoon honey

¹/₂ teaspoon freshly grated orange zest

2 tablespoons freshly squeezed orange juice

8 pheasant breast fillets, about 110g (4oz) each

1 glass of medium-bodied wine such as a New World red

sea salt and freshly ground black pepper

Also good with
chicken breast fillets

This dish is a rich combination of flavours that will assail your senses and make you want to savour every last mouthful. Pheasant fillets are smaller than chicken breast fillets, so we would advise allowing 2 per person. A rather nice touch is to sprinkle some game chips over the pheasant. A traditional accompaniment, these are exceptionally finely sliced pieces of potato that have been pre-soaked to remove the starch, then fried in very hot oil and drained on kitchen paper.

1 Steam the squash, covered, for 5–6 minutes until just tender but not soft. Remove from the steamer.

2 In a frying pan over a fairly high heat, melt the butter with the honey, orange zest and orange juice; stir to combine well. Add the steamed squash, and season with salt and black pepper. Reduce the heat to medium-low, and cook, stirring gently, for 1–2 minutes until the squash is well coated in the orange glaze.

3 Meanwhile, season the pheasant fillets with a little black pepper. In another large frying pan, melt the butter over a medium heat. Put all 8 pheasant fillets in to brown for about 2 minutes on each side. Pour over the red wine, then reduce the heat and simmer gently for a further 10 minutes.

4 Serve hot with the glazed butternut squash, allowing 2 pheasant fillets for each person.

Spanish guinea fowl in garlic and sherry

Serves 4

2 tablespoons good olive oil

4 guinea fowl supremes (breasts with wing attached), skin on, about 200g (7oz) each

12 small potatoes, thinly sliced

3 whole heads of garlic, unpeeled

8 sprigs of fresh thyme

a good splash of amontillado sherry

sea salt and freshly ground black pepper

Also good with
chicken breast fillets

Fresh thyme adds colour as well as flavour (always keep a pot on your windowsill if you don't have a little herb garden on the go), and it is wonderfully evocative of hot, dry holidays in southern Spain. This is quite a versatile meal. You can serve it with a fresh green salad in the summer months, or add winter vegetables when the days are cooler. Pair with a lovely Rioja, to complement the flavours of thyme, garlic and sherry.

1 Preheat the oven to 190°C/375°F/Gas Mark 5.

2 Heat the olive oil in a wide flameproof dish or casserole that will hold the 4 supremes. Season the guinea fowl with salt and black pepper, and brown on both sides for about 7 minutes – just enough to colour, not cook through.

3 Scatter the potatoes over the bottom of the dish or casserole while it is still on the heat. Add the heads of garlic and thyme, and season with salt and black pepper. Stir to coat it all in the juices. Sit the supremes on the top, skin-side up. Add the sherry and bring to the boil.

4 Now put the dish or casserole in the oven, uncovered, for about 1 hour until the guinea fowl is crisp, golden brown and tender. The juices will be absorbed by the potatoes. Serve with whole baby corn on the cob and sugar snap peas.

Slow, slow guinea fowl

Serves 4

4 guinea fowl breast fillets, skin on, about 200g (7oz) each (or supremes – breasts with wing attached)

2 onions, sliced

2 celery sticks, sliced

450g (1lb) carrots, sliced

400ml (14fl oz) chicken stock

1 glass of dry white wine

small handful of fresh tarragon leaves or 1 teaspoon dried

sea salt and freshly ground black pepper

We were approached some years ago by, and became very interested in, the Slow Food Movement. This organisation promotes the use of fresh vegetables and actively encourages slow-grown organic meat without the use of hormones or antibiotics, as well as marketing the concept of buying good, clean and fair products – things very close to our own hearts. This recipe is a great example of taking a wholesome bird and turning it into a hearty meal the old-fashioned way – slowly!

1 Preheat the oven to 180°C/350°F/Gas Mark 4.

2 In a heavy frying pan over a medium-high heat, lightly brown the guinea fowl on both sides for about 7 minutes. Transfer to a casserole, and add the remaining ingredients. Season with salt and black pepper.

3 Roast in the oven for 1½–2 hours until tender. Alternatively, throw everything into a slow-cooker, and switch on!

Guinea fowl hotpot

Serves 4

1 large onion, chopped

1 tablespoon olive oil

1 guinea fowl, about 1.3kg (3lb), cut into 8 pieces

plain flour for dusting

2 garlic cloves, crushed

4 sprigs of fresh thyme

300g (10oz) chestnut mushrooms

400ml (14fl oz) red wine

200ml (7fl oz) chicken stock

12 large waxy potatoes such as Charlotte, peeled but left whole

knob of butter

Also good with lamb

It may seem unusual to put poultry in a hotpot, but guinea fowl does actually do the job on this occasion. It benefits from basting in the sauce, and being sealed under the potatoes to retain the juices and make a lovely gravy. You can use porcini mushrooms for extra flavour, if you like, and serve with red cabbage to follow through on the hotpot theme.

1 Preheat the oven to 220°C/425°F/Gas Mark 7.

2 Sauté the onion in a little olive oil for a few minutes in a large flameproof casserole until soft. Dust the guinea fowl pieces in a little flour, and fry in batches over a high heat until browned. Stir in the garlic, thyme, and mushrooms, and pour in the wine.

3 Bring to a boil, pour in the stock and bring back to the boil. Reduce the heat slightly, and simmer gently for 1¼ hours until the liquid is reduced and meat is cooked.

4 In the meantime, boil the potatoes for 15 minutes, cool and slice thinly. Arrange the potato slices over the top of the casserole, working from the outside in so that they overlap. Dot with a little butter, and bake in the oven for 20 minutes until the potato slices are crisp.

Guinea fowl supremes with tarragon and white wine

Serves 4

4 guinea fowl supremes
(breasts with wing attached),
skin on
large handful of fresh tarragon
or 2 tablespoons dried
60g (2oz) butter
1 glass of dry white wine
300ml (10fl oz) double cream
sea salt and freshly ground
black pepper

Also good with
chicken breast fillets

This recipe is the speciality of a customer of ours, David White, who has now retired from the restaurant trade, but used to own the Stableyard Restaurant in Bangor on Dee.

1 Coat the supremes in the tarragon. Slowly melt the butter in a large frying pan, and seal the supremes on both sides. Pour over the wine and cream, season with salt and black pepper, and cook in this sauce for 20 minutes until firm to the touch. Remove the supremes from pan, and leave to rest in a warm place.

2 To finish, quickly reduce the sauce over a high heat. Serve poured over the supremes, on a bed of wild rice and garnished with some fresh tarragon.

Goat

Goat is one of the most widely eaten red meats in the world, and is cooked and enjoyed across Africa, Asia, South and Central America, some parts of Europe and, more recently, the United Kingdom. We were delighted to come across Chestnut Meats in Cheshire, who produce our kid goats for us. One of the problems with producing dairy animals, whether goat, cattle or buffalo, is that there will always be surplus males, and it is good to be able to resolve this issue in a practical way. Chestnut Meats breeds Boer goats, primarily, which make particularly good meat animals. In Spain, kid goat is known as *cabrito*, and a common term for adult goat meat is 'chevon', from the French *chèvre*. You will find goat meat commonly used in Mediterranean, Middle Eastern, Pakistani, Indian, Mexican and Caribbean cuisines.

ORIGINS
The domestic goat (*Capra aegagrus hircus*) descends from the wild goat of southwest Asia and eastern Europe and is closely related to the sheep; there are more than 300 distinct breeds.

COMMON CUTS
Leg, shoulder, chump, thick rib, steaks, chops, tenderloin or fillet, minced or made into sausage.

TASTES LIKE
Goat is leaner and contains less cholesterol and saturated fat than lamb and beef. It tastes more like mutton than lamb, and long, slow cooking generally produces the best flavour and texture.

BEST WAYS TO COOK
Roasted, barbecued, grilled, casseroles, curries and tagines.

SIGNATURE DISH
Mediterranean kid goat (see pages 90–1).

Kid with red peppers

Serves 4

4 boneless kid goat leg chops,
175–225g (6–8oz) each

juice of 1 lemon

handful of fresh mint
leaves, chopped

handful of fresh
oregano, chopped

1 teaspoon ground cumin

2 tablespoons olive oil

2 red peppers, deseeded and
thickly sliced

2 onions, thickly sliced

sea salt and freshly ground
black pepper

Also good with
pork chops

This is one of the simplest methods of serving kid goat meat
that we have found, making it a popular choice for a week-
night supper dish when you want a change from beef, pork or
lamb – and yet it is also a wonderful option for a dinner party
if you need to produce a quick but impressive main course.
You can keep the chops medium-rare, as they will be nice and
tender. Another option is to barbecue them, in which case you
could skewer the peppers and char-grill them, turning them
over the coals and basting with olive oil as they cook. We're
always up for al fresco!

1 Put the goat in a bowl with the lemon juice, mint, oregano
and cumin. Season with salt and black pepper, and toss well to
coat the meat evenly in the marinade.

2 Heat the grill until hot. Spread the peppers and onions over
a baking tray, and drizzle with the olive oil. Grill until slightly
charred at the edges. Remove from the heat, and keep warm.

3 Now grill your goat chops for about 6 minutes on each side,
depending on their thickness, until crispy and tender. Arrange
on a plate on top of the grilled peppers and onions, and serve
with salad potatoes and fresh mint.

Spiced goat casserole

Serves 6–8

2kg (4¹/₂lb) kid goat
meat, diced

2 tablespoons ground
coriander

2 tablespoons ground cumin

1 tablespoon ground
cardamom

1 teaspoon ground ginger

1 teaspoon pimentón picante
(hot smoked paprika)

1 cinnamon stick

300g (10oz) onion, diced

1 tablespoon minced garlic

100g (3¹/₂oz) carrot, diced

100g (3¹/₂oz) celery, diced

100g (3¹/₂oz) leek, diced

1–2 tablespoons olive oil

200g (7oz) cubed pancetta

200ml (7fl oz) dry white wine

1 x 400g (14oz) can peeled
plum whole tomatoes,
chopped in can

1 bay leaf

veal or light beef stock,
to cover

sea salt and freshly ground
black pepper

Also good with
chicken or diced veal

The wonderful aromas of the spices used here are guaranteed
to have family and friends flocking to see what's cooking.

1 Put the meat in a bowl, and coat with the spices, tossing
gently until evenly mixed. Cover and leave to marinate in
the refrigerator for several hours, preferably overnight.

2 Preheat the oven to 160°C/325°F/Gas Mark 3. In a heavy frying
pan, sweat the onion, garlic, carrot, celery and leek in the oil
for a few minutes. Remove the goat meat to a plate, and add
any marinade spices left in the bowl (including the cinnamon
stick) and the pancetta to the onion mixture; fry for a few
minutes until fragrant. Tip the contents of the pan into a large
flameproof casserole. Increase the heat under the frying pan,
and quickly brown the meat in batches. Add to the casserole.

3 Pour the wine into the frying pan, and bring to the boil. Let
bubble for a couple of minutes, stirring to deglaze, then pour
over the meat in the casserole. Tip in the tomatoes and their
juices, and add the bay leaf and just enough stock to cover the
meat. Bring to the boil, reduce the heat and gently simmer for
a few minutes. Cover with a lid, and transfer to the oven to
braise for 1¹/₂ hours or until tender. Check the seasoning, and
serve with creamy mashed potato and/or date dumplings.

Date dumplings In a large bowl, mix together 250g (9oz) plain
flour, 1 heaped teaspoon baking powder, a pinch of salt, a
good grinding of black pepper, 125g (4¹/₂oz) shredded beef or
vegetarian suet and 2 tablespoons chopped ready-to-eat dates.
Make a well in the centre, and add just enough water to make a
soft dough. With floured hands, shape into 12 balls. Place in
the casserole for the last 20–30 minutes of cooking, turning
once to coat in the spicy gravy; keep the lid on while cooking.

Mediterranean kid goat

Serves 4–6

12 large ripe tomatoes, roughly chopped

about 3 tablespoons olive oil

1 joint of kid goat, on the bone, about 1.5kg (3lb 3oz)

2 glasses of dry white wine

4 onions, sliced

12 garlic cloves, chopped

6 fennel bulbs, trimmed and sliced

2 celery sticks

1 litre (1¾ pints) chicken stock

a large bundle of fresh oregano, thyme and rosemary, all tied together

20 Kalamata olives, pitted and blanched very briefly (for just 10 seconds)

2 tablespoons chopped flat-leaf parsley

sea salt and freshly ground black pepper

For the marinade

60ml (2fl oz) olive oil

2 garlic cloves, finely chopped

grated zest of 1 lemon

2 teaspoons ground fennel

2 teaspoons ground coriander

This is another dish that really benefits from sitting in the refrigerator overnight in a marinade, so plan ahead. The great thing is that you can serve this roast with mashed sweet potato and green vegetables such as beans or curly kale, or it is equally marvellous with a crisp green salad and Jersey or other new potatoes dripping in butter.

1 Mix together all the marinade ingredients, and rub into the meat. Leave to marinate in the refrigerator for at least 4 hours, preferably overnight.

2 Gently simmer the tomatoes in a little olive oil over a low heat until starting to break down; they should be soft, but still holding their shape. You can remove the skins while they are cooking, if you like. Remove from the heat, and set aside. Now relax – nothing will be happening until tomorrow.

3 Preheat the oven to 130°C/250°F/Gas Mark ½. Remove the joint from the marinade, and season with salt and black pepper. Heat 2 tablespoons olive oil in a heavy lidded roasting tin over a medium-high heat. Lightly brown the meat on both sides for a few minutes. Remove to a plate.

4 Gently sweat the onion, garlic, fennel and celery in the same pan for about 10 minutes until starting to caramelise. Tip in the wine and stewed tomatoes, and simmer for about a minute, before adding the chicken stock and bundle of herbs.

5 Return the joint to the pan, cover with a tight-fitting lid and bring to a simmer. It can now gently braise in the oven for as long as you like – any time after 2 hours should see the meat falling off the bone. Garnish with the olives and scatter over the parsley, and serve hot.

Kleftiko parcels

Serves 4

1 boned leg of kid goat, about 750g (1¹/₂lb), well trimmed and cut into bite-sized cubes

75ml (2¹/₂fl oz) extra virgin olive oil

juice of 1 lemon (about 3 tablespoons)

2 teaspoons roughly chopped oregano leaves

2 teaspoons picked thyme leaves

4 garlic cloves, finely chopped

2 beefsteak tomatoes, skinned, deseeded and chopped

175g (6oz) feta or goat's cheese (optional)

4 small bay leaves

sea salt and freshly ground black pepper

Also good with
lamb or mutton chops

Greek *kleftiko* is traditionally made with lamb or goat, and baked whole in a special oven, which often was not much more than a hole in the ground. This makes the meat beautifully moist and tender, and it is a regular feature of holidays and celebrations. This recipe is a variation on the original, as we have diced the goat meat and made up small individual portions, rather than roasting it whole, then carving the joint. We found that this worked really well with kid goat, which does not require the prolonged slow-roasting for which *kleftiko* is renowned.

1 Put the kid meat in a large bowl, and pour over the olive oil. Add the lemon juice, oregano, thyme, and garlic, and season with salt and black pepper. Mix together well, cover and leave to marinate at room temperature for 2 hours or in the refrigerator overnight.

2 Preheat the grill or charcoal barbecue. Line 4 small bowls with a double thickness of foil, allowing it to hang over the edges. Divide the goat evenly among the foil-lined bowls, sprinkling each pile with the tomatoes. Arrange slices of the cheese on top (if using), and stick a bay leaf in each portion.

3 Pinch together the edges of the foil to make well-sealed parcels, remove from the bowls and grill over low-medium coals for 30–40 minutes until the lamb is completely tender and the cheese has begun to melt. Serve hot with crusty garlic bread and a crisp green salad.

Goat in paper

Serves 6

1 boned leg of goat, about
1.35–2kg (3–4¹/₂lb)

6 garlic cloves, halved

2 tablespoons chopped
flat-leaf parsley

2 tablespoons
chopped rosemary

1 tablespoon chopped
oregano or 1 teaspoon dried

¹/₂ teaspoon ground cumin

75ml (2¹/₂fl oz) olive oil

juice of 1 lemon

225g (8oz) graviera cheese or
other hard cheese such as
Gruyère, thickly sliced or grated

sea salt and freshly ground
black pepper

Also good with
boneless leg of lamb

Here, the meat is wrapped in baking parchment so that
the juices steam the meat as it cooks, keeping it tender and
moist. Ideal for a main course when served warm with a crispy
salad, the melt-in-the-mouth goat contrasts wonderfully with
crunchy fresh vegetables – try building up green salad leaves
with tiny raw cauliflower florets, chunky pieces of cucumber,
sliced peppers and celery.

1 Rinse the leg of goat, pat dry with kitchen paper and sit
in a glass or ceramic dish large enough to hold the boneless
leg comfortably. Using a sharp knife, make small slits in the
thickest parts of the leg, and insert the garlic. Sprinkle the leg
with the parsley, rosemary, oregano, cumin and rosemary, and
season with salt and black pepper. Mix together the oil and
lemon juice, and drizzle over the top. Cover and marinate in
the refrigerator for at least 3 hours or preferably overnight.

2 Preheat the oven to 160°C/325°F/Gas Mark 3. Spread out a
sheet of baking parchment large enough to wrap the goat leg,
and rub the paper with a little olive oil. Place the marinated leg
on the oiled paper, and arrange the cheese over the top of the
meat. Roll up the meat, enclosing the cheese, and tie together
in several places with kitchen string to secure. Now wrap the
leg tightly in the paper.

3 Transfer to a shallow pan or roasting tin, and roast in the
oven for 2 hours. Leave to rest in a warm place for 10 minutes,
then cut into slices and serve with a fresh green salad.

Goat tagine with honeyed prunes

Serves 6

1kg (2lb) shoulder of goat, cut into 4cm (1³/₄in) cubes

2 Spanish onions, coarsely grated

3 plump garlic cloves, crushed

4 tablespoons olive oil

large pinch of dried red chilli flakes

¹/₂ teaspoon ground ginger

¹/₂ teaspoon ground cumin

¹/₂ teaspoon paprika

pinch of saffron threads, lightly crushed

2 x 400g (14oz) cans peeled whole plum tomatoes

1 strip of orange zest

2 cinnamon sticks

1 bunch of fresh coriander, chopped

24 large ready-to-eat prunes

3–4 tablespoons clear honey

75g (3oz) blanched almonds, toasted until golden

freshly ground black pepper

fresh mint leaves, to garnish

Also good with
lamb

We think that there is something absolutely delicious about combining opposites in cooking, such as hot with cold, smooth and crunchy, and fruit with meat. The flavour of the prunes is enhanced by the addition of honey, which tempers the stronger flavours of the chilli and ginger. After marinating and slow-roasting in the oven, the goat will be ready to fall apart in your mouth, contrasting with the crunchy garnish of toasted almonds.

1 Put the goat in a glass or ceramic bowl. Add the onions, garlic, oil, chilli flakes, ginger, cumin, paprika, saffron and plenty of black pepper. Stir to coat the meat well. Cover and leave to marinate in the refrigerator for at least 2 hours, preferably overnight.

2 Preheat the oven to 160°C/325°F/Gas Mark 3. Heat a heavy frying pan over a medium heat. Add the goat in batches, and sear on all sides for 10 minutes until evenly browned. Transfer to a tagine or heavy casserole. Tip the remaining marinade into the frying pan; cook, stirring, for 2–3 minutes, then stir into the goat. Add the tomatoes (including any juices) to the casserole, along with the orange zest, cinnamon and half the coriander. Mix well, cover and cook in the oven for 1¹/₄ hours.

3 Meanwhile, put the prunes in a small saucepan with the honey and just enough water to cover, and gently simmer for 10 minutes. Add the prunes and their cooking liquor to the tagine, and cook for a further 15 minutes, sprinkling in the remaining coriander about 8 minutes before the end. Scatter the toasted almonds over the tagine, garnish with mint leaves and serve with couscous.

Hot spicy goulash with kid goat

Serves 4–6

1kg (2¼lb) kid goat meat, cut into 3cm (1¼in) cubes

about 2 tablespoons olive oil

1 large onion

2 green or red bird's-eye chillies, thinly sliced

600ml (1 pint) good beef or veal stock

about ½ bottle red wine such as a heavy claret

1 red pepper, deseeded and thickly sliced

1 yellow pepper, deseeded and thickly sliced

1 green pepper, deseeded and thickly sliced

3 slices dark brown, granary or malted bread, coated with English mustard

2 bay leaves

handful of fresh mixed herbs such as rosemary and thyme, or 1–2 teaspoons dried

a couple of drops of Tabasco sauce, or to taste

sea salt and freshly ground black pepper

Also good with
beef braising steak

This recipe was handed down through the generations to my partner, Ben, who comes from Belgium. On many an occasion we have sat down to enjoy this dish, which for Ben holds fond memories of his grandmother – although she used beef instead of goat. We have tweaked it a little and found it works perfectly with kid goat, which lends itself especially well to braising slowly. It is ideal for setting up in a slow-cooker. Alternatively, set aside a few hours to make it, then reheat when ready to serve. A cautionary note: it is very moreish, and there will be no leftovers!

1 Take the diced meat and, using a little olive oil, brown the meat in a large heavy pan over a medium heat for about 10 minutes. In a separate pan, gently sweat the onion in a little oil for a few minutes until soft and translucent. Add the sliced chillies to the onions, and stir for another minute or so.

2 Tip the onion mixture into the pan with the browned meat, and pour in the stock and red wine. Reduce the heat, and add the peppers. Drop in the slices of bread – they will slowly thicken the goulash as it braises. Add the bay leaves, mixed herbs and Tabasco, and season with salt and black pepper.

3 The goulash can now simmer away gently in the pan for 2½ hours. Alternatively, transfer to a casserole or tagine, and cook in a preheated 180°C/350°F/Gas Mark 4 oven.

4 Finally, check the seasoning, adding a little more Tabasco if needed to give the goulash the required 'kick'. The bread will have softened completely and melted into the goulash, giving it a superb consistency. Serve hot with mashed potatoes or rice to soak up the delicious juices.

Boned leg of kid goat with sherry and honey

Serves 6

250ml (8fl oz) dry sherry such as manzanilla

200ml (7fl oz) clear honey

2 or 3 sprigs of fresh thyme

8 whole cloves

3 star anise

2 cinnamon sticks, broken into pieces

10–15 whole black peppercorns

1 lemon, halved

1 orange, halved

2 tablespoons olive oil

1 boned leg of kid goat, about 1.5kg (3lb 3oz)

Also good with
mutton or lamb shoulder

Remember when you used to take exams and the teachers would say, 'Make sure you read the paper thoroughly before you start!' Well, this recipe is a bit like that. It is not one to be rushed, so allow an extra day for the marinating, as it is vital to the cooking time suggested here.

1 Pour the sherry and honey into a glass or ceramic dish large enough to hold the goat leg comfortably, and add the thyme, cloves, star anise, cinnamon and black peppercorns. Whisk together the ingredients until combined. Squeeze the juice from the lemon and orange halves into the marinade; do not discard the squeezed rinds.

2 Put the goat leg in the dish with the marinade. Tuck in the orange and lemon rinds. After 30 minutes, turn the goat over. Cover with cling film, and marinate in the refrigerator for 24 hours, turning the goat over several times during that time.

3 The next day, remove the goat from the marinade, and preheat the oven to 200°C/400°F/Gas Mark 6. Heat a large roasting pan until hot. Pour in the oil and, when hot, add the goat and sear for 3–4 minutes until browned. Turn the goat over, and brown on the other side.

4 Sit the browned goat joint directly on an oven rack, with a tray underneath to catch the juices. Roast for 35–45 minutes for medium meat. Remove the goat from the oven, and leave to rest in a warm place for at least 10 minutes.

5 Now you can carve and serve this masterpiece with something really Greek – try tiny potatoes roasted in olive oil with fresh rosemary and garlic.

Goat koftas

Serves 4

1 tablespoon coriander seeds
1 tablespoon cumin seeds
1 teaspoon cayenne pepper
$1/2$ teaspoon ground cinnamon
handful of fresh flat-leaf parsley
handful of fresh mint leaves
2 onions, roughly chopped
3–4 garlic cloves, roughly chopped
500g (1lb 2oz) finely minced kid goat
1 large egg
sea salt and freshly ground black pepper

Also good with
lamb mince or mixture of beef and pork

These little fellows are wonderful on the barbecue, adding a touch of Middle Eastern flavour to the usual array of sausages, burgers and steaks, yet they are simple to make beforehand and leave in the fridge until you need them. Bamboo skewers add a touch of the rustic, and are easily available in most supermarkets now, but you can use metal skewers if you like.

1 If using bamboo skewers, soak in cold water for at least 30 minutes, which will help to prevent scorching.

2 Take the coriander and cumin seeds, and grind them with a little salt using a mortar and pestle. If you don't have one, a wooden chopping board and rolling pin will suffice.

3 Put the ground spices in a food processor, along with the cayenne, cinnamon, parsley, mint, onions and garlic. Whizz to a coarse paste. Add the goat mince, and whizz again briefly. Be careful not to purée the meat and turn it into a paste – it should remain quite a nice rough texture.

4 To make the koftas, form the spicy meat mixture around the skewers in a long kebab shape. Grill on a hot barbecue – or indoors if the weather isn't up to it – until golden and cooked through, and serve with some delicious Mediterranean-style dips such as hummus and tzatziki.

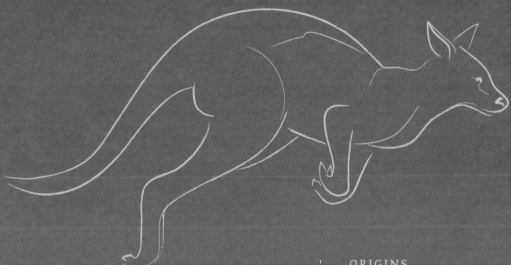

Kangaroo

For more than 40,000 years, indigenous Australians have eaten and survived on kangaroo meat as part of their diet – it has to be the *ultimate* free-range meat! Even today, kangaroos are not domesticated for farming, but instead range freely on grazing land before being harvested for their meat. Even the tail can be used – in soups and casseroles – much like oxtail. Care should be taken not to overcook this tender and succulent meat because of its extremely low fat content. The finer cuts – fillet, loin and rump – can be prepared as steaks or turned into goujons for stir-frying. The steaks are fantastic pan-fried in a really good olive oil with nothing but freshly cracked black pepper and sea salt. Joints should be larded with bacon or covered with foil, to keep the meat moist.

ORIGINS
Large marsupial mammals native to Australia, four species of which are harvested on a commercial basis: the red, eastern grey, western grey and antilopine.

COMMON CUTS
Fillet, saddle, rump, casserole meat, mince.

TASTES LIKE
Gamy and very like venison in texture, colour and flavour, with a slightly different finish on the tongue.

BEST WAYS TO COOK
Stir-fried (medium-rare), pan-fried (rare), char-grilled (rare), roasted, braised.

SIGNATURE DISH
Stir-fried kangaroo with black beans and chillies (see pages 104–5).

Bacon-wrapped kangaroo

Serves 4–6

600g (1lb 5oz) soft dark brown sugar

500ml (16fl oz) soy sauce

1.5kg (3lb 3oz) piece of kangaroo fillet, rolled and banded to form a loin shape

500g (1lb 2oz) streaky bacon rashers

a little white granulated sugar (optional)

Also good with
any other game meat

This is such a simple way of preparing a really delicious and unusual roast. You can substitute any other game meat for the kangaroo, as the bacon wrapping will keep it moist and ensure a succulent result. We have also tried this recipe with venison loin and ostrich fillet, and the results were spectacular.

1 In a small bowl, mix together the brown sugar and soy sauce.

2 Put the kangaroo fillet in a shallow glass or ceramic dish, and pour the brown sugar/soy sauce mixture over the meat. Roll the meat around in the marinade, so that it is well coated. Leave to marinate in the refrigerator for at least 3 hours, preferably overnight.

3 Preheat the oven to 180°C/350°C/Gas Mark 4. Remove the fillet from the dish, and place on a roasting rack set in a roasting tin. Reserve the marinade.

4 Wrap a piece of bacon around the very end of the tenderloin, securing the bacon strip with a cocktail stick. This is a quick way of starting the wrapping process, which you continue until the entire fillet is wrapped in 10 or so bacon 'loops'. Drizzle the remaining marinade over the joint, and baste the loin with the marinade throughout the roasting process.

5 Place the roasting tin on the middle shelf of the oven, and roast for 25–30 minutes for rare; 30–40 minutes for medium. To create a sweet crust on top of the bacon, try lightly dusting the top of the loin with a little white sugar about 10 minutes before the end of the cooking time. Remove to a warm plate, cover loosely with foil and leave to rest for 10 minutes.

6 Serve cut into slices with a lightly tossed salad of rocket, spinach and watercress in the summertime or with roasted sweet potatoes and a medley of green vegetables in the winter.

Kangaroo escalopes in tipsy cream

Serves 4

60g (2oz) butter
4 shallots, finely chopped
2 garlic cloves, finely chopped
4 kangaroo loin fillets, about 170g (6oz) each
1 tablespoon redcurrant jelly
2 tablespoons dry sherry
250ml (8fl oz) single cream

Also good with
beef sirloin (cooked until rare)

Don't you love it when a recipe includes the word 'tipsy'. It generally guarantees that the chef will be able to enjoy a small tipple whilst cooking! Kangaroo meat can be a little sharp in its flavour, which is why we think that it makes a wonderful sausage, but when served as a naked steak it does benefit from the addition of fruit or alcohol. Once again, we would urge you to keep an eye on the temperature and timing while searing your steaks – keep them nice and pink in the centre to ensure that they retain their natural succulence and tenderness.

1 Melt the butter in a saucepan over a low heat, and sweat the shallots and garlic for a few minutes until soft and translucent. Remove with a slotted spoon, and set aside.

2 Increase the heat until the butter is very hot, add the meat fillets and seal on either side. Fry for about 4 minutes, turning only once, then remove to a warm plate, cover with foil and leave to rest while you finish making the sauce.

3 Return the shallots and garlic to the pan, and stir in the redcurrant jelly and sherry. Bring to the boil, stirring all the time. Remove from the heat, and stir in the cream.

4 Arrange the kangaroo fillets on a serving platter, and pour the sauce over the meat. Serve immediately with celeriac mash to soak up that lovely sauce, and some Chantenay carrots and green beans to add colour and texture.

Kangaroo escalopes with anchovy butter

Serves 4

100g (3½oz) butter, softened

12 salted anchovy fillets in olive oil, drained

1 teaspoon freshly squeezed lemon juice

450g (1lb) kangaroo loin fillets, trimmed

a little olive oil

sea salt and freshly ground black pepper

Also good with
beef sirloin or rump steak, venison fillets or ostrich fillets

When we first heard of making an anchovy butter, we thought that it would be so overpowering that it would mask the flavour of any meat – not so! We roped in the services of our lovely Girl Friday, Diane, sending her off home to experiment on her unsuspecting partner, Andy. The results were very surprising. They both thought that the anchovy butter went beautifully with the kangaroo, and would actually work as well with any other red meat such as beef, venison or ostrich.

1 Put the softened butter in a blender or food processor with the anchovies and lemon juice. Season with salt and black pepper, and whizz until well blended. Transfer onto a piece of foil, form into a sausage shape and roll up the foil to make a cylinder of butter. Chill until firm.

2 Cut the kangaroo fillet into 12 thin slices, and brush with a little olive oil. Season lightly with black pepper. Heat a large frying pan until very hot. Add the oiled kangaroo slices, a few at a time, and quickly sear for 1–2 minutes on each side. Do not turn until the first side is properly sealed.

3 To serve, slice the anchovy butter into 12 discs, transfer the meat to a warm serving plate and arrange the discs of butter on top so that they melt over the hot meat. Serve immediately.

Stir-fried kangaroo with black beans and chillies

Serves 4

300g (10oz) baby
bok choy, washed

2 tablespoons groundnut or
vegetable oil

1 teaspoon chopped shallots

2 teaspoons chopped fresh
bird's-eye chillies

1 teaspoon finely
chopped garlic

1 teaspoon chopped fresh
root ginger

2 tablespoons Chinese rice
wine such as Shaoxing

400g (14oz) kangaroo fillet,
trimmed and sliced into
thin strips

1 tablespoon cooked black
beans, washed and drained

150ml (5fl oz) light beef stock

60ml (2fl oz) light soy sauce

1 teaspoon fish sauce such as
nam pla

1 teaspoon freshly ground
black pepper

Also good with
strips of pork fillet

This recipe uses an Asian fish sauce to add flavour and
robustness to the final result. We recommend that you do try
to get hold of a good fish sauce such as nam pla, which can be
found in most Asian supermarkets. The succulent pale green
leaves in this recipe are baby bok choy (also called pak choi),
which can nowadays be commonly found in supermarkets.
They will wilt quickly in the heat of the wok, and that is your
signal that the dish is ready to be whisked to the table.

1 Trim the bok choy leaves, and slice the larger ones in half
lengthways, leaving the stalks attached.

2 Heat some oil in a large wok over a medium-high heat, then
add the shallots, three-quarters of the chillies, three-quarters
of the garlic and the ginger; stir-fry quickly for 30 seconds
until fragrant. Add the rice wine, and reduce until it thickens.
Add the black beans, stock and soy sauce, and bring to the
boil. Simmer for 5 minutes, then tip the contents of the
wok into a bowl. Set aside to keep warm.

3 Carefully wipe out the wok with some kitchen paper.
Add some more oil and, when hot, add the remaining garlic
and chillies, then the kangaroo strips. Toss quickly for a few
seconds over a high heat.

4 Return the warm sauce to the wok, and add the bok choy.
Stir-fry quickly for about a minute until the leaves have just
wilted. Season with the fish sauce and black pepper. Pile onto
the centre of a plate, and serve at once with rice or noodles.

Cornish pasties from Down Under

Serves 4

450g (1lb) ready-prepared shortcrust pastry

450g (1lb) kangaroo mince

100g (3^1/$_2$oz) onions, finely chopped

100g (3^1/$_2$oz) swedes, diced

200g (7oz) potatoes such as Maris Piper, diced

1 egg, lightly beaten, for egg wash

sea salt and freshly ground black pepper

It's a Cornish tradition to personalise the steam vents in the top of your pasties with your initials, but we're not precisely sure what they would do in Australia ...

1 Preheat the oven to 200°C/400°F/Gas Mark 6.

2 Roll out the pastry on a floured work surface, then cut into 4 discs using side plates as guides for the shape. Chill for at least 1 hour.

3 Layer the filling ingredients on the centre of each of the pastry circles, leaving room to seal the edges and seasoning with salt and black pepper as you go. Brush the edges with a little beaten egg, and bring up two sides of the pastry to meet in the middle and form a half-moon shape, pinching together the edges to seal and make that familiar wave over the top. Using a sharp knife, cut two slits in the top of each pasty to allow steam to escape – or embellish with your monogram if you prefer, like Cornish dwellers of old. Brush the tops with a little more of the egg wash.

4 Bake in the oven for about 10 minutes, then reduce the oven temperature to 180°C/350°F/Gas Mark 4, and cook for a further 40 minutes until the pastry is golden. You can always protect your pasties with a loose covering of foil if they are getting a tan too quickly. Serve hot or warm.

Mutton and veal

A significant part of our time working together has been devoted to trying to rekindle interest in the UK veal industry. But we in no way support the crating of veal calves or the old-fashioned veal-rearing methods used on the Continent. Our veal comes from the surplus male calves produced in the dairy industry, reared in welfare-friendly conditions and grown to well over the age of the average chicken or lamb that goes into our food chain. A practical, no-nonsense solution to an age-old problem, this is a natural progression if you want to drink milk – simple as that. Mutton is another classic staple that has fallen out of favour, but is undergoing a renaissance. Although mutton can be available all year, in Britain, the best meat is produced from October to March, when sheep have access to summer and autumn grass and heather, and are able to put on fat.

ORIGINS

Mutton A sheep that is usually more than 2 years old or has reached the end of her useful breeding life.
Rosé veal Meat from young calves (mostly bull calves) slaughtered at 6–8 months.

COMMON CUTS

Mutton is dressed like lamb, while veal is dressed like beef. Two particularly special cuts of veal are escalopes and sliced shin, or shank, which has the bone and marrow left in.

TASTES LIKE

Mutton has a richer flavour than lamb. Rosé veal, which has been out to pasture or fed on cereal, is tender yet full of flavour.

BEST WAYS TO COOK

Mutton Slow-roasting, braises, stews, casseroles.
Rosé veal Pan-frying, grilling, casseroles, pies.

SIGNATURE DISH

Osso bucco (see page 116).

Braised mutton and caper cobbler

Serves 6

1kg (2¼lb) diced leg of mutton

2 celery sticks, halved

3 medium carrots, peeled and cut in half

½ small swede, cut into 12 chunks

6 small onions, peeled but left whole

6 small turnips, scrubbed but not peeled

sprig of fresh rosemary

sprig of fresh thyme

1 litre (1¾ pints) lamb stock made with 2 good-quality stock cubes

10 whole black peppercorns

sea salt

For the cobbler topping

110g (4oz) butter, diced

350g (12oz) self-raising flour

50g (2oz) capers, chopped

handful of fresh flat-leaf parsley, chopped

4 spring onions, finely chopped

2 tablespoons plain yogurt mixed with 75ml (2½fl oz) cold water

1 egg, lightly beaten, for egg wash (optional)

freshly ground black pepper

Several of the United Kingdom's celebrity chefs have put together a collection of recipes to be included in the campaign known as the Mutton Renaissance, which is also promoted by HRH Prince Charles. This particular recipe is courtesy of Brian Turner, CBE, and is a really traditional, hearty meal combining lovely winter root vegetables and delicious leg of mutton.

1 Put the mutton in a large flameproof casserole or pan with all the vegetables and herbs. Pour in the stock, add the peppercorns and season with salt. Bring to the boil, reduce the heat slightly and simmer gently for 1 hour.

2 Preheat the oven to 200°C/400°F/Gas Mark 6.

3 To make the cobbler, rub the fat and flour together using your fingertips until the mixture resembles breadcrumbs. Stir in the capers, parsley and spring onions. Season with black pepper. Add just enough of the yogurt liquid to make a soft, pliable dough.

4 On a floured work surface, roll out the dough until it is 2.5cm (1in) thick. Using a biscuit cutter or a sharp knife, cut into 12 rounds or wedges. Arrange on top of the mutton in the casserole. Lightly brush the top of the cobbler with a little egg wash (if using). Bake in the oven for 20–25 minutes until the cobbler is well risen and golden brown. Serve hot.

Plain roasted leg of mutton

Serves 6

1 leg of mutton, about
2kg (4½lb)
½–1 tablespoon olive oil
2 onions, roughly chopped
about 6 garlic cloves, peeled
and cut in half horizontally
a couple of sprigs of fresh
rosemary
a few sprigs of fresh thyme
400ml (14fl oz) dry white wine
sea salt and freshly ground
black pepper

Also good with
leg of lamb or goat

Slow-cooking is the order of the day with this lovely joint of meat. You will be joining the mutton renaissance once you've discovered the joys of this most traditional of British meats – mutton was a staple of the postwar diet.

1 Preheat the oven to 110°C/225°F/Gas Mark ¼. Season the mutton well with salt and black pepper.

2 Heat the oil in a roasting tin over a medium heat. Add the mutton, and brown on all sides. Add the onions, garlic and herbs, and sauté for a few minutes to lightly brown the onion and garlic. Remove everything from the roasting tin, and set aside. Pour the wine into the tin, and scrape the pan with a wooden spoon to dislodge any bits stuck on the bottom. Return the mutton and vegetables to the roasting tin, cover tightly with foil and roast in the oven for 1 hour.

3 Remove the foil, and carefully add enough water to have about 1cm (½in) of liquid in the bottom of the tin. Continue to cook, uncovered, for 5 hours, adding more water as needed to baste the mutton joint.

4 Remove the mutton from the roasting tin, strain any liquid through a sieve and reserve for the gravy, discarding the herbs and vegetables. Reheat gently if needed.

5 Serve with the usual accompaniments to a Sunday roast, including as many root vegetables as you can for authenticity.

Crusty veal pie

Serves 4–6

30g (1oz) butter

450g (1lb) diced rosé veal

175g (6oz) mushrooms, sliced

30g (1oz) plain flour

300ml (10fl oz) chicken stock

5 tablespoons low-fat
crème fraîche

2 teaspoons wholegrain
mustard

1 teaspoon dried sage

5 slices white bread

1 garlic clove, crushed

60g (2oz) butter

sea salt and freshly ground
black pepper

Also good with
beef braising steak

One of our lovely pie recipes, this holds delicious secrets under the crispy crust. There is something about combining textures when using meat that is simply magical. We also particularly enjoy the addition of wholegrain mustard, which adds a lovely piquancy to the sauce.

1 Melt most of the butter in a heavy pan over a medium heat. Add the veal, and sauté until lightly browned. Tip in the mushrooms, and sauté for a few more minutes until they are starting to soften, then stir in the flour and cook, stirring, for another few minutes. Gradually add the chicken stock and bring to a high heat, stirring all the time. Simmer gently for about 1½ hours until the meat is very tender.

2 Preheat the oven to 180°C/350°F/Gas Mark 4.

3 When the meat is tender, add the crème fraîche, wholegrain mustard and sage. Heat through, season with salt and black pepper, and transfer to an ovenproof dish. Spread the bread lightly with a mixture of the remaining butter and garlic. Cut into triangles, and arrange on top of the veal mixture. Cook in the oven for about 30 minutes until the topping is crisp and browned. Serve hot.

Rich shortcrust veal, mushroom and ale pie

Serves 6–8

For the pastry

500g (1lb 2oz) plain flour

370g (13oz) butter

large pinch of salt

$^{1}/_{2}$ teaspoon baking powder

2 eggs, lightly beaten, plus 1 extra, for egg wash

squeeze of lemon juice

1–2 tablespoons cold water

For the filling

1kg (2$^{1}/_{4}$lb) diced rosé veal steak

250g (9oz) rosé veal kidneys, diced

2 litres (3$^{1}/_{2}$ pints) beef stock

250g (9oz) mushrooms, quartered

generous pinch of chopped fresh oregano

generous pinch of chopped fresh basil

300ml (10fl oz) brown ale

20g ($^{3}/_{4}$oz) plain flour

2 tablespoons vegetable oil

sea salt and freshly ground black pepper

Also good with beef or chicken

I started to write a little introduction for this dish, and looked across at Rachel: 'What can we say about the veal, mushroom and ale pie?' She stared at me and rubbed her tummy. I knew she was casting her mind back to our eating experience a few days earlier. 'Ooooh, yum' was her succinct but apt reply.

1 Heat the oil in a saucepan over a medium-high heat. Add the veal and kidneys, and stir with a wooden spoon, allowing the meat to brown and the juices to ooze from the veal. Continue cooking until all the juices have reduced, then cover with the stock, reduce the heat and simmer for 1 hour until tender.

2 Drain the meat mixture, reserving any liquid. Return the meat to the pan, sprinkle over the flour and cook over a low heat, stirring constantly, for 5 minutes. Add the mushrooms, herbs, beer and enough of the reserved liquid to cover. Season with salt and black pepper, and gently simmer for 30 minutes.

3 Preheat the oven to 180°C/350°F/Gas Mark 4. To make the pastry, process the flour, butter, baking powder and salt to a fine sandy texture. Add the eggs, lemon juice and just enough water that the dough forms into a ball. On a floured work surface, roll out half the pastry until 3mm ($^{1}/_{4}$in) thick. Use to line a lightly oiled 25cm (10in) pie dish or individual dishes.

4 Spoon the slightly cooled meat filling into the pastry shell/s, and moisten the pastry edge with cold water. Roll out the other half of the pastry, and lay across the top of the pie/s. Crimp together the edges to seal, and trim off any excess. Brush the pie top/s with the egg wash, and make an incision or two to allow steam to escape. Bake for 50–60 minutes until golden. Serve hot with mashed potatoes and honey-glazed carrots.

Grilled rosé veal chops with deep-fried sage

Serves 4

4 rosé veal chops
1 tablespoon olive oil
1 tablespoon freshly squeezed lemon juice
sea salt and freshly ground black pepper

For the deep-fried sage leaves
about 36 fresh sage leaves
vegetable oil for deep-frying

Also good with
pork chops

The combination of sage and veal is timeless – the French know all about it. The only tricky part of this recipe is deep-frying the sage leaves, which you may need to practise to get absolutely right. We're looking for crispy, not cremated!

1 First make the deep-fried sage leaves. Wash and dry the sage leaves really well, then drop them in small batches into a pan of hot oil – the oil should be hot enough to sizzle a cube of bread straight away. When you think they are done, remove with a slotted spoon, and drain on kitchen paper. Set aside.

2 Heat a lightly oiled ridged cast-iron grill pan over a medium heat. Grill the veal for about 12 minutes on both sides, turning once. Gently warm the oil and lemon juice in a small pan, and pour this over the chops, garnishing with the fried sage leaves. Serve immediately.

Osso bucco

Serves 4

3 tablespoons plain flour

4 thick slices of rosé
veal shin, bone in

50g (2oz) butter

2 tablespoons olive oil

150ml (5fl oz) dry white wine

450g (1lb) fresh ripe tomatoes,
blanched, skinned and roughly
chopped, or 1 x 400g (14oz)
can peeled whole plum
tomatoes, chopped in can

150ml (5fl oz) veal or
beef stock

sprig of fresh flat-leaf parsley

sprig of fresh thyme

1 bay leaf

sea salt and freshly ground
black pepper

This veal dish originates from Milan, in Italy, but is enjoyed worldwide. Osso bucco is vastly enhanced by the addition of a gremolata at the point of serving, and this is the traditional accompaniment. The gremolata recipe below comes from Judith Hand, of the Torquay International School. This is more than a garnish – it makes a huge difference to the dish.

1 Preheat the oven to 180°C/350°F/Gas Mark 4. Season the flour with salt and black pepper, and use to coat the meat well on both sides.

2 Heat the butter and oil in a casserole over a medium heat. Add the veal and sauté for 12 minutes, turning once, until browned on both sides. Pour in the wine and cook, uncovered, for 10 minutes.

3 Add the chopped tomatoes, including any juices, along with the stock and herbs. Cover and cook in the middle of the oven for 2 hours until the meat is very tender and falls away from the marrow bone in the middle. Serve hot, with gremolata sprinkled over the top. This is delicious served with sautéed potatoes and steamed broccoli.

Gremolata Mix together 1 finely chopped garlic clove, 2 teaspoons chopped flat-leaf parsley and the grated zest of ½ lemon.

Ostrich

Such a special bird, the ostrich is renowned for many things, notably the fact that it is one of the fastest land creatures in the world. Speeds of more than 75km/h (45mph) hour over the African plains have been recorded, and it is the largest living bird species. Ostriches have two toes on their enormous feet. The only direction in which they can kick is forwards, but they can inflict severe injury or even death with their powerful legs. They are incredibly stupid, as we discovered when we farmed them here in the United Kingdom in the 1990s; their brain is only as big as their eye, which makes it quite small. They are, however, very beautiful, and their mating displays are a sight to behold. They also lay the largest egg in the world – a marvel of creamy alabaster-like shell capable of holding the equivalent of 25 hen eggs!

ORIGINS
A member of the Ratite family, this large flightless bird – *Struthio camelus*, to give it its Sunday-best name – is native to Africa.

COMMON CUTS
Ostriches have absolutely no breast meat. For one thing, they have never flown and built up muscle there; secondly, they use their armour-plated breasts to charge and spar against each other. Most of the meat comes from the back of the birds, and the top of the leg or drum.

TASTES LIKE
The texture and initial flavour of beef fillet, with a slight duck or goose aftertaste.

BEST WAYS TO COOK
Pan-fried, char-grilled, stir-fried, roasted, slow-cooked casseroles and braises, burgers and kebabs.

SIGNATURE DISH
Bacon-wrapped ostrich with balsamic red wine sauce (see pages 126–7).

Ostrich stuffed peppers

Serves 4

175g (6oz) long-grain rice

225g (8oz) fresh or ready-made tomato sauce (see below)

1 teaspoon dried oregano

450g (1lb) ostrich mince

1 garlic clove, crushed

4 red peppers

sea salt and freshly ground black pepper

Also good with
a 50:50 mix of beef and pork mince

The bright colours of the peppers used in this dish and the very Italian flavours of oregano and tomatoes are so evocative of sunny climes and lazy lunches. This is a perfect lunchtime snack served with crisp garlic bread, a leafy green salad, an ice-cold beer ... and a view.

1 Preheat the oven to 200°C/400°F/Gas Mark 6. Put the rice in a saucepan with a little salt, and cover with water until it comes 2.5cm (1in) or so above the level of the rice. Bring to the boil, reduce the heat slightly and simmer for 10 minutes only – the rice should not be completely cooked.

2 Meanwhile, in a large mixing bowl, mix together the tomato sauce, oregano, ostrich mince and garlic until well combined. Drain the rice well, and add to the bowl. Mix thoroughly.

3 Cut the tops off the peppers; reserve to use as lids. Deseed the peppers, and arrange cut-side up in a shallow roasting tin. Spoon a portion of the rice mixture into each one, filling each generously and mounding the mixture slightly. Cover with their lids, then loosely cover the tin with baking parchment or foil. Roast in the oven for 45 minutes. Serve immediately.

Fresh tomato sauce To make your own fresh tomato sauce, which tastes much better than shop-bought versions, heat 2 tablespoons olive oil in a pan over a medium heat, and sweat 2 finely chopped garlic cloves for about 5 minutes until soft and starting to caramelise. Add 6–8 roughly chopped and deseeded ripe tomatoes, 1 teaspoon crumbled dried oregano and a small handful of freshly chopped basil leaves. Season with salt and freshly ground black pepper. Simmer gently for at least 20 minutes, stirring occasionally, until the tomatoes have broken down completely and the sauce is thick and rich.

Ostrich and prune casserole

Serves 4

25g (1oz) butter

1 tablespoon vegetable oil

400g (14oz) ostrich rump steak, cut into nice big chunks

2 teaspoons plain flour

1 onion, chopped

1 bouquet garni

2 whole cloves

1/2 x 75cl bottle of full-bodied red wine such as cabernet sauvignon

450g (1lb) ready-to-eat prunes (you can buy the plump foil-wrapped sort already pitted)

150ml (5fl oz) beef or chicken stock

freshly grated nutmeg

sea salt and freshly ground black pepper

Also good with
beef

We recommend serving this casserole with something that will soak up the lovely juices, perhaps mashed potatoes with chives or a timbale of basmati rice. Add some colour with green vegetables such as steamed broccoli and mangetout.

1 Preheat the oven to 180°C/350°F/Gas Mark 4.

2 Heat the butter and oil in a flameproof casserole until very hot. Dredge the ostrich meat chunks in the flour until well coated, and lightly fry until browned. Remove to a warm plate.

3 Sauté the onions in the casserole for about 5 minutes until soft and starting to caramelise. Return the ostrich meat to the pan, and add the bouquet garni, cloves and wine. Dot the prunes over the top.

4 Cover with a lid, and bring to the boil, then transfer to the oven to simmer for 2 hours. By this time the juices should have reached a lovely consistency, but if not you can balance the sauce by removing the meat to a warm plate, then simmering the juices to thicken. Return the meat to the casserole to heat through before serving. Season with a little freshly grated nutmeg, salt and black pepper, and serve hot.

Ostrich al Italia

Serves 2

2 ostrich fillets, about 225g
(8oz) each, diced

1 tablespoon olive oil

1 onion, chopped

1 red pepper, halved, deseeded
and chopped

1 x 400g (14oz) can peeled
whole plum tomatoes

150ml (5fl oz) tomato passata

pinch of sugar

2 teaspoons dried thyme or
oregano

2 garlic cloves, chopped

sea salt and freshly ground
black pepper

Also good with
diced pork or beef

We both really love Italian food (what's not to like!), and it seemed very natural for us to take this recipe and experiment with ostrich meat, as this dish has been a family favourite for years. As everything goes into the pot at the same time, it is also perfect for a Crock-Pot or slow-cooker. The fillet, although tender, will tighten on cooking initially and therefore needs to be slowly braised to be able to relax again. By the end of the process, it should be melt-in-the-mouth.

1 Preheat the oven to 180°C/350°F/Gas Mark 4.

2 In a flameproof casserole, gently fry the diced ostrich in the olive oil for a few minutes until browned. Remove to a warm plate. Now add the onion and red pepper to the casserole, and sweat for about 5 minutes until soft.

3 Return the meat to the casserole with the onion and red pepper, and add the tomatoes (including any juices), passata and a pinch of sugar. Crumble in the thyme or oregano, and add the garlic. Season with salt and black pepper.

4 Cover with a lid, and cook in the oven for 1½ hours. Serve hot on a bed of penne pasta cooked until al dente.

Really wild kebabs

Serves 4

500g (1lb 2oz) game sausages such as ostrich, venison or springbok

8 ready-to-eat prunes

1 tablespoon olive oil

sea salt and freshly ground black pepper

Also good with
any other savoury sausage

It's a really good idea to take a sausage apart and utilise the sausagemeat in a different way – mostly because the flavouring and seasoning have already been done for you. You can often find pork sausagemeat easily, but the more unusual meats are much harder to source in this form. This recipe morphs the sausages into kebabs in a twinkling, and the result is not only delicious, but also innovative and fun.

1 Soak 4 bamboo skewers in cold water for 30 minutes. Preheat the oven to 200°C/400°F/Gas Mark 6.

2 Split the sausage skins, remove all the sausagemeat and roll it into 12 small meatballs; discard the skins. Thread a meatball, then a prune, onto each soaked skewer, so that each one has 3 meatballs and 2 prunes on it.

3 Heat the oil in a frying pan over a medium heat, and gently brown the kebabs for a few minutes. Transfer to a baking tray, and roast in the oven for 6 minutes or until cooked through. Serve hot.

Chilli stir-fried ostrich

Serves 4

1 tablespoon vegetable oil

2 small fresh red chillies, finely sliced

2 garlic cloves, crushed

5cm (2in) piece of fresh root ginger, finely chopped

450g (1lb) ostrich fillet, very thinly sliced into 5cm (2in) strips

275g (10oz) green beans, finely sliced

2 teaspoons sugar

1 tablespoon light soy sauce

2 teaspoons sesame oil

2 teaspoons rice vinegar

Also good with
strips of chicken fillet

We've said it a lot, but honestly – ostrich rules the fast-food world. You need only 10 minutes to arrive at this nutritious, tasty result. Vary the vegetables or add a couple more, such as julienne carrots and fresh asparagus spears. You can't go wrong. We always love to use little tiny 'oak trees' of broccoli in a stir-fry, to add texture and colour, but the vegetable world is your oyster.

1 Heat the oil in a large wok over a medium heat. Add the chilli, garlic and ginger, and stir-fry for 2 minutes.

2 Add the ostrich meat, and continue to stir-fry for 2 minutes, then add the beans and stir-fry for a further 4 minutes or until the beans are just tender.

3 Push the ostrich and beans to the edges of the wok, add the remaining ingredients and stir well. Return the ostrich and beans to the centre of the wok, and toss to coat and heat through. Serve immediately with fluffy white rice or noodles.

Little and large ...

Serves 4

2–3 tablespoons olive oil

8 pigeon breasts

2 ostrich steaks, about
175g (6oz) each, halved

1 onion, diced

1 garlic clove, crushed

1 dessert apple, peeled, cored,
and diced

4 streaky bacon rashers, diced

150ml (5fl oz) dry white wine

150ml (5fl oz) chicken stock

175g (6oz) mushrooms, sliced
(optional)

sea salt and freshly ground
black pepper

... or pigeon and ostrich casserole. Our neighbour Pauline Speake, of Wem, Shropshire, suggested that this casserole was very suitable for the slow-cooker, but it can also be gently braised in the oven. We were so taken with the contrasting choice of meats that we had to include it in our collection.

1 Preheat the oven to 180°C/350°F/Gas Mark 4. If using a slow-cooker, prepare according to the instructions.

2 Heat the olive oil in a heavy pan over a fairly high heat. Leaving the pigeon breasts whole, seal all the meat and set aside on a warm plate. In the same pan, soften the onion, garlic and apple for a few minutes, and set aside. Now fry the diced bacon until golden brown, but not crisp.

3 Put all the ingredients into either a lidded casserole or a slow-cooker, and season well with salt and black pepper. Add the wine and stock, and cook in the oven for 1½–2 hours; allow 5–6 hours in the slow-cooker. About 15 minutes before serving, if needed, thicken the sauce by adding the mushrooms. Serve hot with the vegetables of your choice ... delicious.

Bacon-wrapped ostrich with balsamic red wine sauce

Serves 4

1 x 1kg (2¼lb) boneless ostrich joint

a few sprigs of fresh thyme, leaves picked

a few sprigs of fresh rosemary, leaves picked

10 rindless streaky bacon rashers or thin pancetta slices

2 tablespoons virgin olive oil

1 onion, sliced

1 carrot, diced

1 leek, trimmed and diced

2 tablespoons balsamic vinegar

150ml (5fl oz) full-bodied red wine such as cabernet sauvignon

300ml (10fl oz) beef stock

freshly ground black pepper

Also good with
boneless rabbit

You can treat ostrich as you would beef fillet, but with a little more care in larding, whatever form that takes. You can choose to wrap in bacon, as here, or pour olive oil over it and wrap in foil, or even thread pancetta through the outer layer. The bacon keeps the joint sealed and protects it from drying out, as ostrich is not a marbled meat and is not self-basting. This process produces a great result.

1 Preheat the oven to 230°C/450°F/Gas Mark 8.

2 Sit the joint on a chopping board. Season with the thyme and rosemary leaves, by pressing the edge of a sharp knife into the joint to create little pockets all over, then spearing the flesh with the herbs. Add a good grinding of black pepper.

3 Wrap the joint in the bacon or pancetta, overlapping the rashers or slices, and secure with cocktail sticks. Drizzle with the olive oil, and place in a roasting tray with the onion, carrot and leek. Roast in the oven for 15 minutes, then reduce the oven temperature to 200°C/400°F/Gas Mark 6, and cook for a further 30 minutes.

4 Remove the meat to a plate when cooked (hopefully it will still be pink in the centre), cover with foil and leave to rest in a warm place.

5 Add the balsamic vinegar, wine and stock to the pan, and stir through to deglaze. Strain into a clean pan, and discard the vegetables. Reduce the sauce until it has thickened slightly. Slice the joint, and pour the sauce over the top. Serve with game chips and mashed root vegetables such as swede, carrots or sweet potato.

Fillets of ostrich with nutmeg creamed spinach

Serves 2

2 large handfuls of fresh
spinach leaves

a little freshly grated nutmeg

2 tablespoons double cream

liberal splash of extra virgin
olive oil

2 ostrich fillet steaks, about
175g (6oz) each

sea salt and freshly ground
black pepper

Also good with
beef fillet

One of the most delicious ways to cook ostrich fillet steaks is simply to pan-fry them. We recommend a good extra virgin olive oil – a liberal splash into the pan – and heating the oil until just smoking. Always cook ostrich fillet steaks rare or, at the most, medium-rare, to retain the tenderness and natural succulence. Being extremely low in fat, they can be dry and tough if cooked for too long, which is criminal.

1 Wash the spinach in a colander, removing any tough stems. Put in a saucepan, and cook until just wilted. Blend or process to a purée, and season with a little freshly grated nutmeg, salt and black pepper. Stir through the cream. Reheat gently when ready to serve – do not allow to boil.

2 Heat a splash of olive oil in a heavy frying pan or ridged cast-iron grill pan or griddle until smoking hot. Season the steaks with salt and black pepper. When the oil is hot, sear the steaks for about 8 minutes on each side; a little longer for medium-rare. Remove to a warm plate, and leave to rest for 5 minutes.

3 Serve surrounded by the creamed spinach, with sautéed or lyonnaise potatoes to add some texture.

Mini Yorkshire puddings topped with ostrich fillet

**Serves 6 as a
starter or canapé**

1 x 500g (1lb 2oz) roasting
joint of ostrich rump

olive oil

2 glasses of red wine such
as merlot

sea salt and freshly ground
black pepper

fresh horseradish cream,
to serve

6 sprigs of fresh flat-leaf
parsley, to garnish

For the Yorkshire puddings

goose fat or beef lard

450g (1lb) self-raising flour

6 eggs, plus 1 egg white

300ml (10fl oz) milk

Also good with
roast beef

We first saw this idea at the launch of Clarissa Dickson
Wright's book *Sunday Roast*. Clarissa was demonstrating
the carving of a huge side of roast beef for her puddings.
We decided then and there that it would work just as well
with thin slices of roasted ostrich rump.

1 Preheat the oven to 190°–200°C/375°–400°F/Gas Mark 5–6.
Rub the ostrich joint all over with olive oil. Place in a roasting
tin, and season with salt and black pepper. Roast in the oven
for no more than 10 minutes per kg or 20 minutes per lb –
you want a rare result to experience the ostrich at its best.
Remove from the oven, and leave to rest in a warm place.

2 To make the jus, place the roasting tin over a low heat, and
pour in the red wine. Bring to a simmer, scraping up any bits
stuck to the bottom of the pan with a wooden spoon. Allow
to reduce a little, then strain and keep warm.

3 To make the Yorkshire puddings, increase the oven
temperature to 220°C/425°F/Gas Mark 7. Put a little goose fat
or lard in each hole of a 6-hole large muffin tray, and sit in
the oven until piping hot. In a bowl, whisk together the flour,
6 eggs and milk until smooth. Stir through the egg white (to
make your puddings extra light and fluffy). Reduce the oven
temperature to 200°C/400°F/ Gas Mark 6, carefully pour the
batter into the holes of the heated tray and bake the puddings
in the oven for about 10 minutes until risen and golden.

4 Thinly slice the ostrich, and fold onto the centre of the
Yorkshire puddings. Top each one with a dollop of horseradish
cream. Finish off with a drizzle of the red wine jus and a
sprig of fresh flat-leaf parsley. Serve hot.

Ostrich with mushrooms in a creamy sauce

Serves 4

2–3 tablespoons olive oil

1 onion, chopped

1 garlic clove, chopped

4 ostrich fillet steaks, about 175g (6oz) each

2 glasses of dry white wine

60g (2oz) butter

225g (8oz) mixed mushrooms, sliced

2 garlic cloves, chopped

150ml (5fl oz) double cream

4 teaspoons wholegrain mustard

sea salt and freshly ground black pepper

Also good with
guinea fowl or beef sirloin

This recipe is often to be found on restaurant menus, served with pork or over a sirloin steak, but we have adapted it for ostrich fillets and it works really well. The ingredients used don't overpower the flavour of the meat, and the creamy piquancy of the sauce is a stroke of genius.

1 Heat 2 tablespoons olive oil in a frying pan over a medium heat. Add the onion, and sauté for 3–4 minutes until soft. Add the garlic, and sauté for a further minute or so. Remove to a bowl, and set aside.

2 Add a little more oil and the butter to the pan. When it is bubbling, quickly sear the ostrich steaks until golden brown on both sides, then reduce the heat and let them sizzle for about 8 minutes on each side until medium-rare. Remove to a warm plate, and leave to rest for 5 minutes.

3 Pour about a glass of wine or maybe a bit more into the pan, and deglaze, using a wooden spoon to scrape up any bits from the bottom. Let bubble for a few minutes until it reduces and thickens. Set aside to keep warm.

4 Heat some more olive oil in a clean pan, add the mushrooms and sauté for 3–4 minutes until starting to brown. Add the garlic, and sauté for 30 seconds or so until the garlic turns white and opaque. Stir in the cream, mustard and a glass of wine. Season with salt and black pepper. Leave to simmer for 6–8 minutes until the liquid has reduced slightly.

5 Serve the steaks on a bed of the mushrooms, with the red wine sauce drizzled over. Accompany with creamed potatoes to soak up the juices, and add some texture and crunch with steamed broccoli florets tossed with toasted sunflower seeds.

Hare

Rabbit

Rabbit and hare

'Run rabbit, run rabbit, run, run, run ...' There are many species of rabbit and hare found throughout the world, from the Arctic tundra to near-desert grasslands and shrub. You may not know, or care, that they are from the family Leporidae, in the order Lagomorpha. There is no doubt, however, of their part in our culture and literature, from their representation in folklore and mythology around the world, to Beatrix Potter's Peter Rabbit stories and the wonderful White Rabbit and March Hare of Lewis Carroll's *Alice's Adventures in Wonderland*. Lower in fat and cholesterol than chicken, rabbit is one of the healthier meats, and is something of a blank canvas when it comes to adding other flavours, colours and texture. The hare is a much larger and more solitary creature by nature.

ORIGINS
Both rabbits and hares are small- to medium-sized mammals in the family Leporidae; there are around 50 species in total.

COMMON CUTS
A 'saddle' of rabbit or hare is the loin of the animal, from the front legs up to where the hindquarters begin, minus the head. Rabbit and hare are often sold cut in half, with the hind legs separate from the saddle.

TASTES LIKE
Rabbit is a mild and tender meat, and is quite versatile. Hare has a stronger, gamier flavour.

BEST WAYS TO COOK
Braised; in pies, stews and casseroles; joints coated in breadcrumbs and deep-fried.

SIGNATURE DISH
Stuffed saddle of rabbit or hare (see pages 136–7).

Crispy rabbit bake

Serves 4

500g (1lb 2oz) diced rabbit

30g (1oz) plain flour, seasoned
with sea salt and freshly
ground black pepper

2 tablespoons olive oil

75g (2¹/₂oz) smoked streaky
bacon rashers, chopped

2 onions, cut into wedges

150ml (5fl oz) pale ale

150ml (5fl oz) beef stock

1 tablespoon Dijon mustard

1 tablespoon wine vinegar

2 teaspoons soft brown sugar

pinch of salt

2 carrots, sliced

2 eggs, beaten

2 tablespoons milk

2 slices white bread, crusts
removed

100g (3¹/₂oz) button
mushrooms, trimmed
and halved

freshly ground black pepper

chopped flat-leaf parsley,
to garnish

Also good with
chicken

Tender pieces of rabbit in rich ale gravy, topped with little
crispy triangles of bread – the smoked bacon really comes
through too – make a very tasty dish for any occasion. We
prefer to use diced rabbit for this recipe, so that nothing
gets in the way of mopping up those juices.

1 Preheat the oven to 180°C/350°F/Gas Mark 4. Toss the rabbit
in the seasoned flour until well coated; reserve any leftover
flour to thicken the gravy.

2 Heat the oil in a pan over a medium heat, and sauté the
pieces of rabbit and bacon until well browned; transfer to a
casserole. Fry the onions in the same oil for a few minutes
until lightly browned and starting to caramelise, then sprinkle
with any remaining seasoned flour. Gradually add the ale and
stock, and bring to the boil. Stir in the mustard, vinegar, sugar
and a pinch of salt, and season with black pepper. Add the
carrots, and pour the contents of the pan over the rabbit and
bacon in the casserole. Cover tightly, and cook in the oven
for about 1¹/₂ hours.

3 In a small bowl, stir together the eggs and milk. Cut the
bread into squares or triangles, and dip into the egg and milk
mixture. Increase the oven temperature to 200°C/400°F/Gas
Mark 6. Remove the lid from the casserole, gently stir through
and check the seasoning, then tip in the mushrooms. Arrange
the soaked bread on top of the casserole, and return the oven,
uncovered, for about 30 minutes until crisp and lightly
browned. Serve sprinkled with chopped parsley.

Traditional hunter's pie

Serves 4–6

2 tablespoons olive oil

675g (1½lb) diced mixed game such as venison, pheasant, partridge, rabbit and pigeon, cut into 2.5cm (1in) cubes

2 red onions, sliced

1 garlic clove, crushed

120g (4oz) streaky bacon rashers, chopped

120g (4oz) chestnut mushrooms, cleaned and sliced

30g (1oz) plain flour

1 tablespoon redcurrant jelly

grated zest and juice of 1 orange

300ml (10fl oz) chicken stock

300ml (10fl oz) red wine such as a nice burgundy

1 bay leaf

340g (12oz) ready-prepared puff pastry

1 egg, lightly beaten, for egg wash

sea salt and freshly ground black pepper

If you can, choose a rustic-looking pie dish for making this – it will match the robust flavours and textures of the filling. I particularly like to use my ornamental pie raiser, which is a blackbird raising its head to the sky – a nice touch, I think.

1 Heat a tablespoon of the oil in a large heavy pan over a fairly low heat, and fry all of the game in batches until well browned. Remove from the pan, and set aside.

2 Heat the rest of the oil in the same pan, and cook the onions for 5 minutes until starting to soften. Add the garlic, bacon and mushrooms, and cook for another 2–3 minutes. Stir in the flour, and cook for 2 minutes until it forms a nice paste.

3 Season well with salt and black pepper, and stir in the redcurrant jelly, orange zest and juice. Pour over the stock and wine, and add the bay leaf. Bring to the boil, return the game to the pan and simmer gently for about 1 hour until the meat is tender. Allow to cool slightly while you preheat the oven to 200°C/400°F/Gas Mark 6.

4 To assemble the pie, pile the game and any accumulated juices into a pie dish. On a floured work surface, roll out the pastry to make a lid to cover the pie, allowing a little extra to make a 'collar' to attach to the dish. Trim a strip about 2.5cm (1in) wide from the pastry, and lightly wet the rim of the dish with a little water. Secure the pastry collar around the edge of the dish, and sit the pastry lid on top, crimping together the edges to seal. Decorate with the trimmings, and use a sharp knife to cut a steam vent in the lid. Glaze with the egg wash.

5 Bake in the oven for 20 minutes, then reduce the oven temperature to 180°C/350°F/Gas Mark 4. Cook for a further 20 minutes until the pastry is golden and risen. Serve hot.

Rabbit with calvados

Serves 4

30g (1oz) butter

1 tablespoon olive oil

60g (2oz) streaky bacon
rashers, chopped

200g (7oz) onion, chopped

2 rabbits, 600–800g
(1lb 5oz–1³/₄lb) each,
skinned and jointed

2 sprigs of fresh thyme

6 or 7 juniper berries, crushed

60ml (2fl oz) calvados

60ml (2fl oz) port or red
wine such as our favourite,
a burgundy

sea salt and freshly ground
black pepper

Also good with
lamb steaks

Produced in the Basse-Normandie region of France, calvados
is a wonderful golden apple brandy that has usually been aged
for several years in oak barrels. If you cannot get your hands
on calvados, use another brandy or cider instead.

1 Preheat the oven to 180°C/350°F/Gas Mark 4.

2 In a deep flameproof casserole, heat the butter and oil over
a medium heat, and sweat the onions and bacon for about a
minute until soft. Remove the onion and bacon to a plate and
keep warm, and brown the rabbit joints on all sides in the
residue for a further 8–10 minutes.

3 Return the onion and bacon to the casserole, and add the
thyme and crushed juniper berries. Gently warm the calvados
in a small high-sided pan. Pour over the rabbit in the casserole,
and carefully flambé until the flames have died away, then add
the port or red wine and 250ml (8fl oz) water to moisten.
Season with salt and black pepper. Cover tightly, and cook in
the oven for about 1 hour.

4 Remove from the oven, and leave to stand for 10 minutes
before serving. Serve with mashed potato, carrots and green
vegetables or red cabbage, or try it with rich brown lentils
and glazed carrots – because rabbits love carrots!

Stuffed saddle of rabbit or hare

Serves 2

2 slices Serrano ham

1 saddle of rabbit or hare, 800g–1kg (1^3/$_4$–2^1/$_4$lb), boned, plus the kidneys (cleaned and halved)

4 tablespoons olive oil

1 carrot, diced

2 celery sticks, diced

4 tablespoons dry white wine

1 tablespoon butter

sea salt and freshly ground black pepper

For the stuffing

100g (3^1/$_2$oz) black pudding

about 2 tablespoons double cream

Also good with
chicken breasts

After some experimenting, we found that this recipe works equally well with either hare or rabbit, even though hare is a much gamier, darker meat. If you can, persuade your butcher to bone out the saddle for you, although it is not as difficult as it sounds if you have a sharp knife and a little patience. Most of all, serve this dish only to someone who deserves the effort!

1 Prepare the stuffing for the rabbit by removing the skin from the black pudding. Put the black pudding in a small bowl, and mash with the cream. Blend until soft and spoonable.

2 On a clean work surface, overlap the ham slices so that they are slightly wider than the rabbit fillet. Lay the fillet on top, and season well with salt and black pepper. Spread the stuffing mixture evenly over the fillet, then roll up the ham to encase the rabbit and stuffing. Secure in place with bands or skewers.

3 Heat the oil in a large heavy pan over a fairly high heat, and add the rolled fillet. Sauté for 5 minutes or until brown and crisp. Toss in the carrot and celery, and fry for 2–3 minutes. Add the kidneys, and fry for 1 minute on each side. Remove the pan from the heat. Put the rabbit – including the kidneys – on a board to rest, and spoon the carrot and celery into a bowl.

4 Put the rabbit pan back on the heat, splash in the wine and stir with a wooden spoon, scraping up any bits stuck on the bottom. Tip the carrot and celery back into the pan, stir in the butter, add the kidneys and just heat through.

5 To serve, slice the rabbit into 6 pieces, 3 on each plate, and pour over the contents of the pan. Serve with some lovely steamed green vegetables.

Game casserole

Serves 4

2 tablespoons olive oil

500g (1lb 2oz) diced mixed game, including rabbit or hare

2 onions, sliced

1 garlic clove, crushed

450ml (15fl oz) red wine such as a nice bordeaux

1 tablespoon tomato purée

2 teaspoons Worcestershire sauce

100g (3½oz) pitted prunes (either ready-to-eat or soaked overnight)

1 bay leaf

1 teaspoon cornflour, to thicken

300ml (10fl oz) beef or vegetable stock (optional)

100g (3½oz) button mushrooms, trimmed and halved

sea salt and freshly ground black pepper

To garnish

6 dry-cured streaky bacon rashers, made into rolls (see right)

a few sprigs of fresh flat-leaf parsley

Also good with
beef braising steak

We love the combination of rich-tasting, tender meats that make a mixed-game casserole, such as pigeon, pheasant, venison and rabbit or hare. You can dice and freeze fresh meat trimmings from different meals you've prepared previously, and combine them yourself in this dish.

1 Preheat the oven to 160°C/325°F/Gas Mark 3. Heat the oil in a flameproof casserole, and fry the mixed game, stirring occasionally, until browned and sealed all over. Add the onions and garlic, and cook for a few minutes, stirring frequently.

2 Pour in the wine, and bring to the boil. Let bubble for a couple of minutes until the alcohol evaporates. Stir in the tomato purée and Worcestershire sauce, and add the prunes and bay leaf. Season with salt and black pepper, and stir through. Cover tightly and cook in the oven for about 2 hours.

3 Blend the cornflour with a little water to make a paste, and stir into the casserole sparingly, adding only as much of the stock as is needed. Tip in the mushrooms, and stir through. Discard the bay leaf, and return the casserole to the oven for 15 minutes until the mushrooms are cooked.

4 Garnish with the bacon rolls and parsley, and serve hot with either fluffy rice or creamed potatoes with nutmeg.

To make the bacon rolls Take the dry-cured bacon rashers, and cut off any rind with kitchen scissors. Stretch out evenly on a board using the back of a knife – this will make the bacon more even and easier to roll. Roll up each rasher lengthways. You can always thread them on to skewers prior to cooking, to stop them unrolling (or use cocktail sticks). Grill until crisp and brown. Remove the skewers or cocktail sticks (if using).

Red deer

Reindeer

Venison

While researching this chapter, we were surprised to learn that 'venison' used to be the term used for the meat of deer, antelopes, goats, wild pigs and hares that were hunted and killed for the table. Nowadays, we associate the term simply with the meat of deer, whether hunted or farmed. In the United Kingdom, the three main types of deer used are the red deer (*Cervus elaphus*), fallow deer (*Dama dama*) and roe deer (*Capreolus capreolus*). The caribou (*Rangifer tarandus*), or reindeer, is also used for venison. The imposing stag, or hart, with his glorious head of antlers, gazing royally over his domain, is as iconic an image as that of tiny fawns with their white-spotted backs nestling in the undergrowth. Venison's healthy attributes have long made it a popular food source in Europe and elsewhere, and that popularity is spreading.

ORIGINS
Members of the Cervidae family found variously in the wild across Europe, Asia and North America.

COMMON CUTS
Mostly hindquarter, saddle and diced; the loin and haunch make deliciously tender steaks, with diced leg casseroling beautifully and the trimmings producing flavoursome sausages.

TASTES LIKE
A dark red meat with a robust but not necessarily stronger flavour than beef, venison is wonderful with red wine and sharp fruits such as juniper or cranberries.

BEST WAYS TO COOK
Pan-frying, grilling, roasting, casseroles and stews.

SIGNATURE DISH
Rack of venison with forest mushrooms (see pages 142–3).

Sticky baked venison sausages

Serves 4

12 large venison sausages
3 tablespoons wholegrain
mustard
3 tablespoons clear honey
2 teaspoons paprika
grated zest and
juice of 1 lemon

Also good with
wild boar sausages or
a good pork variety

Often more readily available than other game meats, venison has even made it onto the supermarket shelves in the past 10 years, and nothing has proved as popular as the venison sausage. The rich, dark meat lends itself superbly to this form of eating, whether it's just a plain venison sausage or married with cranberries, wild mushrooms or black pepper. This simple method of baking sausages turns a mid-week supper into something quite special and different, especially if you are using an unusual sausage such as venison or wild boar.

1 Preheat the oven to 200°C/400°F/Gas Mark 6.

2 Mix together the honey, mustard, paprika, lemon juice and zest. Prick the sausages, and toss in the honey mustard mixture. Put in a roasting tin, and roast in the oven for about 30 minutes until browned all over and cooked right through, turning from time to time while they are cooking.

3 Serve hot with baked jacket potatoes, split and daubed with butter and fresh parsley.

Spicy winter venison casserole

Serves 6

1kg (2¹/₄lb) diced venison

60g (2oz) plain flour, seasoned with sea salt and freshly ground black pepper

about 2 tablespoons olive oil

225g (8oz) baby onions or shallots, peeled but left whole

1 white or brown onion, finely sliced or chopped

3 garlic cloves, crushed

2 tablespoons sun-dried tomato purée

125ml (4fl oz) red wine vinegar

1 bottle (75cl) of red wine such as cabernet sauvignon

2 tablespoons redcurrant jelly

a few sprigs of fresh marjoram

4 bay leaves

2 tablespoons Tabasco sauce

6 juniper berries, crushed

600ml (1 pint) beef stock

450g (1lb) celeriac, cut into chunks

450g (1lb) turnips, cut into chunks

Also good with
beef braising steak

This is a real winter warmer, spicy and full-bodied, and the venison produces a lovely rich gravy, especially if you add the full bottle of wine as suggested. Experiment using any of the game meats – they all go well with the ingredients used in this recipe. The baby onions or shallots provide interesting texture and sweetness. And, if you make this casserole in the summer months, when celeriac and turnips are out of season, opt for celery and carrots instead.

1 Toss the meat in the seasoned flour. Heat a little oil in a large flameproof casserole, and brown the meat (in small batches if necessary) over a medium heat. Remove and set aside. Add a little more oil, and sauté the baby onions or shallots until lightly golden and starting to caramelise. Remove and set aside. Now add the white or brown onion, and sweat for about 5 minutes until soft and transparent. Add the garlic, and sauté, stirring, for 30 seconds until it turns white and opaque.

2 Stir in the tomato purée, cooking slowly over a medium heat. Pour in the vinegar and wine, and bring to the boil. Simmer for 10 minutes. Add the jelly, marjoram, bay leaves, Tabasco and juniper berries. Return the meat to the casserole, and pour in the stock. Bring to the boil once again, then reduce the heat slightly and gently simmer for about 1 hour.

3 Preheat the oven to 180°C/350°F/Gas Mark 4. At the end of simmering time, remove the meat and baby onions or shallots from the casserole. Strain the liquid, and return to the pan; discard the seasonings. Put the meat and baby onions back in the casserole, along with the celeriac and turnips. Bring back to the boil, cover and transfer to the oven to cook for another 45 minutes. Serve with baked jacket potatoes.

Rack of venison with forest mushrooms

Serves 8

1.2 litres (2 pints) beef stock

$1/_2$ leek, green part only, chopped

2 shallots, chopped

1 small carrot, chopped

1 tomato, chopped

$1/_2$ bunch of fresh flat-leaf parsley, leaves picked

125ml (4fl oz) port or red wine

2 teaspoons tomato purée

1 rack of venison (8 ribs, or about 1kg/2$1/_4$lb)

1 tablespoon Dijon mustard (optional)

60–75g (2–2$1/_2$oz) seasoned dried breadcrumbs (optional)

60ml (2fl oz) olive oil

225g (8oz) mixed exotic mushrooms (such as oyster, shiitake and portobello), sliced

sea salt and freshly ground black pepper

chopped flat-leaf parsley or watercress, to garnish (optional)

Also good with
rack of lamb

Make a pal of your local butcher, and persuade him to 'French rack' a loin of venison for you – or try it yourself. It basically means separating and trimming down the ribs, and makes the joint much more presentable. We used forest mushrooms to accompany this dish, as their texture and almost perfumed flavour complements the venison loin. The whole recipe is deliciously decadent, and perfect for a special occasion.

1 Put the stock, leek, shallots, carrot, tomato and parsley in a very large saucepan, and whisk in the port or red wine and the tomato purée. Bring to a slow boil, reduce the heat slightly and simmer for 2 hours, or until the sauce is reduced to about 750ml (1$1/_4$ pints). Strain and discard the solids. Keep warm until needed.

2 Preheat the oven to 220°C/425°F/Gas Mark 7. Put the venison on a rack in a roasting pan, and roast for 25 minutes until medium-rare. Remove the venison from the oven, and set aside. (If you would like to add a crust, brush the Dijon mustard over the roasted venison. Pat on the seasoned breadcrumbs, and return the venison to the oven until the crumbs are lightly golden and toasty.)

3 Meanwhile, heat the oil in a heavy frying pan, and add the mushrooms. Sauté briefly until starting to brown, then season with salt and black pepper.

4 To serve, pour about 60ml (2fl oz) sauce on each of 8 serving plates, gently reheating it beforehand if needed. Place 2 slices of the venison on each plate, on top of the sauce. Garnish with the fresh parsley or watercress (if using), and serve with the sautéed mushrooms. A truly impressive dish.

Herbed venison roast with cranberry and raisin relish

Serves 6–8

1.5–2kg (3$\frac{1}{4}$–4$\frac{1}{2}$lb) venison roasting joint

1–2 tablespoons dried mixed provençal herbs such as basil, thyme, rosemary, oregano, sage and marjoram (use herbes de Provence if you have some)

6–8 streaky bacon rashers

cranberry and raisin relish, to baste (see below right)

Also good with
whole chicken or guinea fowl

The relish used here for basting can easily be made ahead and is such a good idea as an accompaniment for venison, combining as it does the sharpness of citrus and cranberries with the sweetness of raisins and sugar. Of course, the bonus is that, once you have made it, you can keep it refrigerated in an airtight jar for up to a month and use it alongside other meats such as gammon or ham, or chicken or turkey as well.

1 Preheat the oven to 200°C/400°F/Gas Mark 6. Rub the joint all over with the herbs, then wrap it in the bacon; tie securely with kitchen string. Place on a rack in a shallow roasting pan.

2 Purée a little of the cranberry and raisin relish, and use to baste the venison. Roast in the oven, allowing 20 minutes per kg for rare and 30 minutes per kg for medium-rare.

3 Serve thinly sliced on stylish dinner plates, with further lashings of the delicious relish.

Cranberry and raisin relish Put 350g (12oz) seedless Muscat or other raisins, 500ml (16fl oz) freshly squeezed orange juice, 60ml (2fl oz) freshly squeezed lemon juice, 250ml (8fl oz) water and 110g (4oz) sugar in a large stainless-steel or other non-reactive saucepan. Bring to the boil over a high heat, stirring to dissolve the sugar. Reduce the heat, and leave to simmer for 10 minutes. Add 350g (12oz) cranberries and 1 tablespoon grated orange zest. Return to the boil, and simmer for a further 10 minutes until the liquid barely covers the solid ingredients; be careful not to cook too long, or it will set hard. Pour into a hot sterilised jar with a tight-fitting lid, seal and leave on a wire rack or folded tea towel to cool. It will keep in the refrigerator for up to a month.

Medallions of venison with port and cranberries

Serves 4

250ml (8fl oz) chicken stock

250ml (8fl oz) beef stock

125ml (4fl oz) ruby port

90ml (3fl oz) cranberry sauce
made with whole berries

3 tablespoons butter

8 venison medallions,
90–100g (3–3½oz) each,
preferably cut from the
striploin

sea salt and freshly ground
black pepper

Also good with
lamb cutlets

This is a very quick and simple way to create a rich sauce for venison, and using medallions from the loin gives great results every time. The fillet on a deer is extremely small, and so we recommend using striploin to achieve equal-sized medallions. If the portion sizes are equal, the meat will cook evenly, and you won't be giving one guest a rare steak and another one rather well done! Do keep your eye on them, though, and remember the golden rule: undercook rather than overcook.

1 Pour the chicken and beef stocks into a small heavy pan, and stir to combine. Simmer over a medium heat for about 15 minutes until reduced in volume by half. Add the port, and reduce the liquid by half again; about 15 minutes. Whisk in the cranberry sauce, and simmer for 4 minutes or so until the sauce has thickened slightly. Whisk in 1 tablespoon of the butter, season with salt and black pepper, and keep cooking until nice and glossy. Keep warm until needed.

2 Sprinkle the venison medallions with salt and black pepper. Melt the remaining 2 tablespoons butter in a large non-stick frying pan over a high heat. When it is foaming, add the meat; sear for about 2 minutes on each side for medium-rare. Remove to a warm plate, and leave to rest for about 5 minutes.

3 Arrange 2 venison medallions on each plate, and drizzle the sauce over and around the meat. Serve immediately.

Serving suggestion It is rather nice to serve the medallions with garlic mashed potatoes and something colourful with a crisp texture, such as sugar snap peas or runner beans.

Game pâté

Makes 1.5kg (3lb 3oz) pâté

1.5kg (3lb 3oz) diced game
such as venison, pigeon,
rabbit etc.

1 small glass of brandy

1 teaspoon salt

$1/2$ teaspoon freshly ground
black pepper

1 teaspoon ground allspice

1 teaspoon juniper berries

small handful of fresh
thyme leaves

small handful of fresh flat-leaf
parsley leaves

2 garlic cloves

250g (9oz) onions, chopped

60g (2oz) butter

1 egg, beaten

2 glasses of dry white wine

4 tablespoons fresh
breadcrumbs

250g (9oz) streaky
bacon rashers

Also good with
chicken livers, but omit the
allspice and juniper berries
to make a mild pâté

This pâté is lovely as either a starter or light lunch, served with relishes and salad. A nice touch, we always think, is to make your own Melba toasts to serve alongside. Alternatively, go rustic when serving as a main course for lunch, and serve with thick slices of hot French bread and beetroot salad.

1 Mince or finely chop the diced game, and put in a large bowl with the brandy. Grind up the salt, spices, herbs and garlic, and work the mixture well into the meat. Leave to marinate in the refrigerator overnight.

2 The next day, preheat the oven to 160°C/325°F/Gas Mark 3. In a small pan, gently sweat the onions in the butter for 10 minutes until soft and starting to caramelise. Add to the marinated meat along with the egg, wine and breadcrumbs.

3 Line a suitable pâté dish or terrine with the bacon rashers, leaving the ends hanging over the edges of the dish to fold over and cover the top of the pâté. Pack the meat mixture into the middle, and fold over the bacon ends.

4 Cover with foil, and put in a roasting tray; carefully add water to the tray until it comes about halfway up the sides of the dish. Bake in the oven for 2–3 hours until the sides are pulled away from the pâté dish and the juices run clear. Leave to chill overnight with a weight on top. Eat within 3 days.

Serving suggestion To make the Melba toast, simply take a few slices of white bread, and carefully slice each one through horizontally to make 2 really thin slices. Cut into smaller squares if you wish, and toast until dry and golden. Arrange 3 or 4 of the crispy toasts on each plate with a couple of slices of the pâté and perhaps a side salad of rocket and spinach with cherry tomatoes.

Angostura venison cobbler

Serves 4–6

500g (1lb 2oz) venison mince
a little olive oil
1 large onion, sliced
2 carrots, peeled and diced
300ml (10fl oz) beef stock
$1^1/_2$ tablespoons angostura bitters
1 tablespoon tomato purée
2 teaspoons cornflour
sea salt and freshly ground black pepper

For the cobbler topping
175g (6 oz) self-raising flour
40g ($1^1/_2$ oz) butter
$^1/_2$ teaspoon dried mixed herbs
1 egg, beaten
2 tablespoons milk
a few sesame seeds (optional)

Also good with
any type of mince such as lamb or a mixture of beef and pork

Angostura bitters have never been put to a better use. Not something we always have in the cupboard but, once you use them in this recipe, we're sure that you'll experiment with them in other cooking – even the humble shepherd's pie benefits. The cobbler topping is quite filling, so this makes a good family meal as it satisfies the hungriest of teenagers, hard-working gardeners or little people hungry from school.

1 Preheat the oven to 180°C/350°F/Gas Mark 4.

2 Fry the venison gently in a heavy pan until browned, adding a couple of drops of oil if necessary. Add the onion and carrots, and continue cooking for a few minutes.

3 Pour in the stock, and add the angostura bitters and tomato purée. Season with salt and pepper, and bring to the boil. If necessary, blend the cornflour with a little cold water to make a paste, and add to the pan and cook until thickened. Tip the contents of the pan into a heavy casserole, cover and cook in the oven for 20 minutes.

4 To make the cobbler topping, sift the flour into a bowl and rub in the fat with your fingertips until the mixture resembles fine breadcrumbs. Season with salt and black pepper, and stir in the herbs. Bind together with the beaten egg and enough milk to form a softish dough. Pat out the dough on a floured work surface until about 1cm ($^1/_2$in) thick, and use a biscuit cutter to cut into 4cm ($1^1/_2$in) rounds.

5 Remove the casserole from the oven, and increase the oven temperature to 190°C/375°F/Gas Mark 5. Arrange the rounds of dough in an overlapping circle around the top of the casserole. Brush with milk, and sprinkle with sesame seeds (if using). Return the casserole to the oven, and bake, uncovered, for about 20 minutes until the topping is well risen and golden.

Carbonnade of venison

Serves 6

a little olive oil or beef dripping, depending on how healthy you want to be

1.1kg (2½lb) stewing or braising venison, diced

3 onions, sliced

2 teaspoons soft brown sugar

2 tablespoons plain flour

2 garlic cloves, crushed with a little sea salt

300ml (10fl oz) beer

60ml (2fl oz) beef or chicken stock

1 teaspoon malt vinegar

1 bouquet garni

4 juniper berries, crushed

1 large baguette, cut into slices 5mm (¼in) thick

about 2 tablespoons wholegrain mustard

freshly ground black pepper

Also good with
ostrich or braising beef

This recipe was originally handed around between our friends in the 1980s, although it was then intended for beef, rather than venison. It is the sort of dish that is easily prepared in advance – say, in the morning for the meal that evening. Simply stop at the end of step 3. Later, preheat the oven half an hour before you wish to serve the carbonnade, then add the slices of baguette as in step 4 and reheat until ready to serve. We like to serve this with simple steamed vegetables such as broccoli, carrots and new potatoes.

1 Preheat the oven to 180°C/350°F/Gas Mark 4.

2 Heat the oil or dripping in a flameproof casserole over a medium heat until smoking hot. Fry the venison in batches until browned. Remove and set aside to keep warm.

3 Reduce the heat, and add the onions to the pan or casserole. Gently sauté for a few minutes until soft and transparent. Stir in the brown sugar.

4 Return the meat to the casserole, and sprinkle over the flour. Stir through for a few minutes. Add the garlic, beer, stock, vinegar, bouquet garni and juniper berries. Bring to the boil, stirring to combine, then cover and transfer to the oven to cook for 2–2½ hours. (Alternatively, leave to simmer slowly on top of the stove, although you will still need to finish off the next step in the oven.)

5 Take the slices of baguette, and spread wholegrain mustard on one side of each slice. Sit mustard side-up on top of the casserole. The slices will float if you have a lot of gravy – don't worry! Place in the oven for another 20 minutes or so until the bread is crisp and golden. Serve hot.

Caribou roast

Serves 4–6

plain flour for dredging

2kg (4½lb) roasting joint of caribou

600ml (1 pint) beef, chicken or veal stock or water

1 packet onion soup mix

1.35kg (3lb) onions, sliced

drizzle of olive oil

sea salt and freshly ground black pepper

Also good with
pork shoulder or leg

This is a delicious take on the traditional Sunday roast. It roasts well in the oven, but you could also use a slow-cooker, which is a really simple way to produce a warming roast dinner while appearing to be totally in control of your life. The caribou will make its own gravy as it cooks – most helpful.

1 Preheat the oven to 180°C/350°F/Gas Mark 4; if using a slow-cooker, follow the instructions for a roast of this size.

2 Season a little flour with salt and black pepper, and use to lightly coat the roast. Put the caribou in a roasting pan, drizzle with olive oil and put the pan on the stovetop over a medium heat. Brown the roast all over, then add enough of the stock or water to cover. Sprinkle with the onion soup mix, and arrange the onion slices over and around the meat.

3 Roast in the oven, covered, for 3½ hours, or in the slow-cooker for the required time. (To be even more prepared, add some roasting or jacket baking potatoes to the oven about 1 hour before the end of the cooking time.)

4 Remove the caribou from the oven or slow-cooker, and season the onion gravy to taste. Serve cut into slices with the onion gravy poured over the top, big fat roasted or jacket potatoes and honeyed carrots.

Caribou tournedos Rossini

Serves 4

4 slices white bread, crusts removed

60g (2oz) butter

1 tablespoon olive oil

4 caribou tournedos, about 200g (7oz) each

4 thick slices of smooth pâté (Brussels or chicken liver work well)

2 tablespoons port

1 tablespoon brandy

1 tablespoon madeira

175ml (6fl oz) beef, chicken or veal stock

sea salt and freshly ground black pepper

Also good with
beef

Extremely rich and delicious, this recipe is for a really special occasion. It is usually prepared with beef filet mignons, but caribou is equally good and just as tender.

1 Preheat the oven to 180°C/350°F/Gas Mark 4.

2 Cut the slices of bread into circles a little larger than the circumference of the tournedos so that they can sit on them easily – use kitchen scissors! Heat half of the butter and a little of the oil in a frying pan over a fairly high heat. Add the bread, and fry on both sides until golden brown. Drain on kitchen paper, and place on a heatproof serving platter.

3 Meanwhile, heat the remaining butter and oil in another large frying pan until sizzling hot. Season the caribou with salt and black pepper, then add to the pan and sauté for 4 minutes on each side. Remove from the pan with tongs, place each on top of a round of the fried bread and place in the oven to keep warm.

4 Add the pâté to the pan, and sauté briefly just to warm through. Remove from the pan with tongs, place 1 slice on each of the tournedos and return to the oven to keep warm.

5 Pour the port, brandy and madeira into the same pan, and bring to the boil, using a wooden spoon to scrape up any bits in the bottom of the pan. Continue to boil until reduced by half, then add the stock, bring back to the boil and continue to boil rapidly for about 5 minutes to reduce again.

6 To serve, pour the sauce over the top of the tournedos – it's almost good enough to drink.

Caribou steaks with cabernet cherry sauce

Serves 4

4 caribou steaks, about
200g (7oz) each
2 garlic cloves, crushed
sea salt and freshly cracked
black pepper

Cabernet cherry sauce

2 glasses of red wine such
as cabernet sauvignon or a
good burgundy
3 tablespoons balsamic vinegar
4 whole cloves
8 whole black peppercorns
1 bay leaf, torn into
small pieces
225g (8oz) fresh or canned
black cherries, rinsed
1–2 teaspoons sugar (optional)

One of our favourites – we've mentioned it before, but we are suckers for fruit and alcohol. On a visit to family in Belgium, we were served a traditional dish of meatballs, stewed cherries and those wonderful Belgian chips. The combination was so gorgeous that it was not a huge leap to experiment with the rather sweet meat of caribou on our return. The addition of cabernet was, well, an afterthought while we were cooking. But it works!

1 Rub the caribou steaks evenly all over with the garlic. Sprinkle with sea salt and a good grinding of black pepper. Set aside until ready to grill or pan-fry – the choice is yours.

2 To make the sauce, put the wine and balsamic vinegar in a saucepan, and bring to the boil. Using a small piece of muslin, make a small package of the cloves, peppercorns and bay leaf, tying together with kitchen string. Add the bundle to the wine mixture, and allow to reduce for about 15 minutes.

3 While the wine is reducing, pit the cherries. Chop and add to the wine mixture. Cover and cook over a medium-high heat for about 10 minutes until tender. (This time can be reduced by about half if using canned cherries.) Season with salt and black pepper, adding the sugar to balance the flavours if needed. The sauce should be deep and robust, but not too sweet.

4 While the sauce is cooking, grill or pan-fry the steaks for 3–4 minutes on each side for medium-rare. Remove to a warm plate, and leave to rest for 5 minutes.

5 To serve, remove the spice bundle from the sauce. Arrange the steaks on individual plates, and spoon over the sauce.

Wild boar

In days of old, the wild boar (*Sus scrofa*) lived and bred successfully in the United Kingdom, until it was hunted to extinction sometime in the seventeenth century. After this, the beast was mainly found in Eastern European countries such as Hungary and Germany, as well as in France and around the Mediterranean, but is now quite prevalent in Australia, the United States, South America and New Zealand as well. Happily, herds of boar can once again be seen in the British Isles, having been reintroduced by farmers looking to diversify. There have even been sightings of feral wild boar that have escaped from farms and taken once again to the forests in England's south. A group of wild boar is called a 'sounder', which is a very attractive collective noun; the boarlets are rather beautiful, being light brown and stripey.

ORIGINS
Ancestor of the domestic pig that you see in the fields and farms of Britain and elsewhere today.

COMMON CUTS
All the cuts familiar from pork; wild boar prosciutto is a delicacy, while shoulder or leg roasting joints are often used at traditional celebrations such as Christmas.

TASTES LIKE
... pork used to taste, prior to the era of pale, bland and intensively farmed convenience-packed food.

BEST WAYS TO COOK
Roasted, barbecued, casseroles, pan-fried, cured as bacon.

SIGNATURE DISH
Apricot, garlic and thyme roasted haunch of wild boar (see page 154).

Apricot, garlic and thyme roasted haunch of wild boar

Serves 8

1 wild boar joint,
about 2kg (4½lb)

6–8 dried apricots, each
cut into about 3 strips

6–8 garlic cloves, peeled and
each cut into 3 strips

25g (1oz) fresh thyme, broken
into smaller sprigs

150ml (5fl oz) sherry vinegar

5 or 6 allspice berries, freshly
ground

sea salt and freshly ground
black pepper

For the jus
1 large carrot, chopped
2 celery sticks, chopped
1 onion, finely chopped
1 garlic clove, finely chopped
1 glass of red wine
300ml (10fl oz) stock
1 tablespoon tomato purée

Also good with
shoulder or leg of pork

This is a real bobby-dazzler for presentation – how exciting
to produce this joint for your family or dinner guests, and
carve each delicious slice in front of them.

1 Preheat the oven to 200°C/400°F/Gas Mark 6.

2 Trim any excess fat from the haunch, leaving an outside
layer, and reserve for the gravy. Trim a little of the meat
away also, reserving this for the gravy too. Using a sharp knife,
make incisions in the joint in about 15 places. Stuff each one
with some slices of apricot, garlic and a few sprigs of thyme.
Drizzle the sherry vinegar over the boar, and sprinkle over the
ground allspice. Season generously with salt and black pepper.
Sit the boar haunch on a rack set over a suitable roasting tray.

3 Roast the boar for 1¼–1½ hours until golden brown and
cooked through. Baste frequently with any of the juices caught
in the tray. Remove to a board, and rest in a warm place for
10–15 minutes before carving.

4 Pour any juices from the roasting tray into a small jug;
reserve. Sit the roasting tray over a gentle heat, and add the
reserved fat and meat trimmings. Sauté for 2–3 minutes until
well browned. Add the carrot, celery, onion and garlic, and
sauté for a further 2–3 minutes until softened. Deglaze with
the red wine, using a wooden spoon to lift off any of the nice
sticky sediment in the tray. Finally, add the stock, tomato
purée and reserved juices. Simmer gently until reduced by
half. Pass the jus through a fine sieve, and serve over the
wild boar. Marvellous!

Wild boar steaks with oregano

Serves 4

1 tablespoon olive oil

4 wild boar loin steaks, 175–225g (6–8oz) each

1 onion

2 garlic cloves, crushed

1 teaspoon finely grated lemon zest

150ml (5fl oz) chicken or vegetable stock

1 x 400g (14oz) can peeled whole plum tomatoes, chopped in can

1 tablespoon chopped oregano

sea salt and freshly ground black pepper

Also good with
pork steaks or chicken fillets

If you combine these ingredients – tomatoes, oregano, garlic and lemon zest – you will always get a light combination of flavours that is evocative of warm Italian evenings in Rome or Florence ... and wild boar carries this sauce so well.

1 Heat the oil in a large frying pan over a fairly high heat. Arrange the steaks in a single layer, and sear for 2 minutes on each side until browned, then transfer to a warm plate.

2 Using the same pan, sweat the onion, stirring frequently, for 5 minutes until soft and transparent. Add the garlic, chopped oregano and lemon zest. Cook, stirring occasionally, for about 1 minute.

3 Reduce the heat to low, and return the steaks to the pan. Tip in the stock and tomatoes, including any juices. Simmer for 15–20 minutes until the sauce is slightly thickened. Remove from the heat, season with salt and black pepper, and serve.

Serving suggestion **Try serving the steaks with hunks of fresh crusty bread in a rustic French way, to soak up the lovely juices, accompanied by fresh-picked runner beans.**

Sausage sandwich with style

Serves 2

2–3 tablespoons olive oil

4 wild boar, Stilton and spring onion sausages (or whatever game sausages you can find)

1 large onion, sliced

2 tablespoons French mustard such as Dijon

2 tablespoons clear honey

1 ciabatta loaf

It takes only a little imagination and a few extra minutes to turn a very ordinary sausage sandwich into something you might find in a chic little bistro. You can ring the changes by using a baguette instead of ciabatta, if you like. Or add a splash of syrupy balsamic vinegar and a little soft brown sugar to the onions in place of the honey.

1 Pour some olive oil into a frying pan over a medium heat, and slowly cook the sausages for about 15 minutes. Remove to a warm plate, add the onions to the pan and sauté for about 10 minutes until caramelised.

2 Stir in the mustard and honey, then return the sausages to the pan to warm through.

3 Slice the ciabatta, and toast 4 pieces. Pile the sausage and onion mixture onto the ciabatta with the sauce of your choice, such as tomato ketchup or HP.

Italian-style wild boar loin steaks

Serves 4

1 tablespoon olive oil

4 wild boar loin steaks, about 175g (6oz) each

1 onion, finely chopped

2 garlic cloves, crushed

1 tablespoon chopped rosemary leaves, plus extra, to garnish

1 teaspoon grated lemon zest

1/4 teaspoon crushed dried chillies (optional)

150ml (5fl oz) chicken stock

1 x 400g (14oz) can whole peeled plum tomatoes, chopped in can

sea salt and freshly ground black pepper

Also good with
pork chops

Thanks are due to Jeannie's partner, Ben, and his chilli addiction, for it was he who slipped the crushed chillies into this particular recipe for a spectacular added zing. Nothing will be lost, however, if you prefer to omit them and keep to the classic combination of lemon and rosemary.

1 Heat the oil in a large frying pan until just smoking. Arrange the steaks in a single layer, and sear for 2 minutes on each side until browned, then transfer to a warm plate.

2 Using the same pan, sweat the onion, stirring frequently, for 5 minutes until soft and transparent. Add the garlic, rosemary, lemon zest and crushed chillies (if using). Cook, stirring occasionally, for a further minute.

3 Reduce the heat to low, and return the steaks to the pan. Pour in the stock, and tip in the tomatoes and any juices. Simmer for 10–15 minutes until the steaks are no longer pink in the middle and the sauce is slightly thickened. Remove from the heat, season with salt and black pepper, and garnish with a few small sprigs of extra rosemary. Serve with chunks of fresh crusty bread or rosemary and garlic roasted potatoes.

Gin- or brandy-flamed wild boar escalopes

Serves 4

4 wild boar loin steaks,
175–225g (6–8oz) each
a few juniper berries, crushed
2 tablespoons olive oil
1 tablespoon rowan or
redcurrant jelly
8 paper-thin slices of orange
75ml (2½fl oz) gin or brandy
sea salt and freshly ground
black pepper

Also good with
venison loin steaks

We prefer to use gin in this recipe because of the inclusion of juniper berries, but, having run out of gin on one occasion, we can honestly say that brandy works just as well.

1 Sandwich the steaks between 2 large sheets of cling film, and pound with a meat mallet or the side of a rolling pin until thin and evenly flattened into escalopes. Sprinkle with a few crushed juniper berries, and season with salt and black pepper.

2 Heat the oil in a heavy frying pan over a very high heat. Quickly sear the escalopes in the hot oil, then transfer to a warm plate. Brush with a thin layer of the rowan or redcurrant jelly, and garnish with the paper-thin slices of orange.

3 Add a little water to the frying pan, and mix in the pan juices, using a wooden spoon to scrape up any bits on the bottom. Now for the exciting bit. This always causes a stir if you can do it in front of your guests. Gently warm the gin or brandy in a large ladle or small high-sided pan, carefully ignite, then pour it over the pan juices and stir gently. Tip the whole lot, while still flaming, over the steaks. Serve immediately – or as soon as the flames have disappeared.

Serving suggestion Try serving with creamy garlic mashed potatoes and steamed green vegetables such as broccoli, mangetout and sugar snap peas.

Toad in the hole

Serves 4

For the toad
2 onions, sliced
8 thick boar, venison or other game sausages
olive oil
French wholegrain mustard

For the batter
110g (4oz) plain flour
pinch of sea salt
4 free-range eggs, beaten
300ml (10fl oz) milk
2 tablespoons chopped fresh chives or thyme leaves
3 tablespoons vegetable oil or beef dripping
freshly ground black pepper

Also good with
plain old pork sausages

If you use a nice, rich gravy saved from the Sunday roast, it turns a humble mid-week supper dish into a glorious feast.

1 To make the batter, sift the flour and salt into a large bowl. Make a well in the centre, and break the eggs into it. Gradually whisk the eggs into the flour. Slowly add the milk until the batter is thick enough to coat the back of a spoon. Stir in the thyme, and season with black pepper. Cover and leave to stand for 30 minutes.

2 Preheat the oven to 220°C/425°F/Gas Mark 7.

3 Heat the oil in a pan over a medium heat, add the onions and sweat for about 5 minutes until soft but not coloured. Spoon into the bottom of a roasting dish.

4 Fry the sausages over a medium heat until golden brown all over. Brush them with a little mustard, and set aside. Add the oil or beef dripping to the onions in the roasting dish, and cook in the oven for 5 minutes or until the dripping is hot and almost smoking. Add the sausages to the dish, and carefully pour over the batter. Immediately return the dish to the oven, and bake for 35–40 minutes until well risen and golden. If the batter begins to brown too much, reduce the oven temperature to 190°C/375°F/Gas Mark 5.

5 If you are serving the toad in the hole with gravy left over from a Sunday roast, reheat gently until warmed through. Serve immediately the toad in the hole comes out of the oven, with the gravy for pouring over.

Baked wild boar steaks

Serves 4

4 thickly sliced wild boar loin
steaks, 175–225g (6–8oz) each

60g (2oz) fresh breadcrumbs

pinch of soft brown sugar

finely grated zest of 1 orange

2 egg whites

freshly grated nutmeg, to taste

1 glass of dry white wine

a little butter

sea salt and freshly ground
black pepper

Also good with
veal chops or steaks

What a simple but delightful way to serve wild boar. The
paste seals in the juices and keeps the steaks moist, while also
crisping up to contrast nicely with the tender meat inside.

1 Preheat the oven to 190°C/375°F/Gas Mark 5.

2 In a small bowl, mix together the breadcrumbs, sugar,
orange zest, nutmeg, egg white and enough wine to make
a thick paste. Season with salt and black pepper.

3 Place a small knob of butter on top of each steak, then coat
each steak in the paste. Roast in the oven for 15–20 minutes.
Serve hot with mashed sweet potato and asparagus spears.

Stuffed wild boar tenderloin

Serves 4

500g (1lb 2oz) wild boar tenderloin

2 streaky bacon rashers

2 red onions, roughly chopped

2 sprigs of fresh rosemary

3 tablespoons olive oil

2 glasses of dry white wine

150ml (5fl oz) meat or vegetable stock

For the stuffing

30g (1oz) butter

2 shallots, finely chopped

$1/2$ tablespoon finely chopped sage leaves

110g (4oz) baby spinach leaves, shredded

30g (1oz) ham, chopped

60g (2oz) fresh breadcrumbs

1 egg, beaten

$1/2$ teaspoon freshly grated nutmeg

Also good with
veal or pork

This simple method of 'butterflying' a piece of meat to make it flat and easy to stuff and roll brings enormous pleasure to simple folks like us – it's a bit like having special powers. You can apply the procedure to any type of rolled boneless joint or even to a single chicken or other poultry breast fillet.

1 Preheat the oven to 180°C/350°F/Gas Mark 4.

2 Slice open the tenderloin lengthways, cutting two-thirds of the way through. Open it up, and pound the meat gently with a mallet or the side of a rolling pin to flatten and widen so that it can be stuffed. If necessary, take a similar slice not quite through the meat on each side; this 'butterflies' the joint and makes more room for stuffing.

3 To make the stuffing, melt the butter in a small frying pan over a medium heat, and sweat the shallots with the sage for about 10 minutes. Add the spinach, cook until just wilted and remove from the heat. Add the remaining stuffing ingredients. Spread the stuffing along the centre of the butterflied tenderloin, patting it down firmly. Roll up the meat, and tie in place with kitchen string at about 4cm (1¾in) intervals.

4 Lay the meat in a roasting tin, cover with the bacon rashers and surround with the red onions and rosemary. Finally drizzle it with the olive oil. Roast in the oven for 35–40 minutes, basting occasionally. Once cooked, remove the meat to a warm plate, cover with foil and leave to rest for about 5 minutes.

5 Discard the onions and rosemary from the roasting tin, and deglaze the pan over a medium heat with the wine. Add the stock, and boil rapidly until the mixture is reduced by half, then strain. Cut off the string from the boar, and slice the meat on the diagonal. Serve with the gravy.

Wild boar, honey and thyme sausages in cider gravy

Serves 4

1 x 340g (12oz) pack of
wild boar, honey and
thyme sausages
2 onions, halved and sliced
2 garlic cloves, finely chopped
150ml (5fl oz) cider
1 teaspoon fresh thyme leaves
2 teaspoons wholegrain
mustard
4 teaspoons butter, melted
2 teaspoons plain flour
sea salt and freshly ground
black pepper

Also good with
pork and apple sausages

Take one new member of staff (Diane), give her some sausages to take home to try … and, hey presto, a lovely new recipe for an easy supper dish.

1 Preheat the oven to 190°C/375°F/Gas Mark 5.

2 Fry the sausages in a pan over a medium heat for 8–10 minutes until nicely browned. Remove and set aside.

3 Using the same pan, sauté the onions and garlic for a few minutes until soft and beginning to colour. Return the sausages to the pan, and pour over the cider. Stir in the thyme and mustard, and season with salt and black pepper.

4 Transfer the contents of the pan to a flameproof casserole, and roast in the oven for 40 minutes.

5 To finish, mix together the butter and flour to make a roux, and – after taking out the sausages and onions, and setting them aside to keep warm – add the roux to the gravy and return to the heat, stirring rapidly. As the sauce thickens, check the seasoning and adjust, then pour over the sausages and onions. Serve hot.

Serving suggestion This is delicious with celeriac mash and seasonal vegetables.

Cutlets of wild boar with fresh herbs

Serves 4

4 wild boar cutlets or steaks, 175–225g (6–8oz) each

2 tablespoons wine vinegar

2 tablespoons olive oil

1–2 tablespoons single cream or Greek-style yogurt

small handful of fresh lovage leaves, plus extra to garnish

handful of fresh chives, chopped, plus extra to garnish

handful of fresh flat-leaf parsley, chopped, plus extra to garnish

sprig of fresh mint, plus extra to garnish

60g (2oz) butter

sea salt and freshly ground black pepper

Also good with
chicken breast or thigh fillets

There is nothing to compare with the pleasure of using ingredients that have been home-grown or produced. Even something as simple as a window box of herbs can contribute to some really successful but simple meals – this recipe serves as a perfect example.

1 Pack the cutlets or steaks into a dish, and sprinkle with wine vinegar and olive oil so that they are barely covered. Add some lovage leaves, a sprig of mint, some chopped chives and parsley. Leave to marinate for at least 1 hour, turning occasionally. Drain the meat, and reserve the marinade.

2 Melt the butter in a large pan over a quite a high heat, and sear the cutlets or steaks on both sides for 10 minutes, before reducing the heat and cooking more gently for a further 10 minutes. Transfer to a plate, and set aside to keep warm.

3 Pour the reserved marinade into the pan, with all the herbs, and gently cook for a minute to absorb all the pan juices. At the last minute, check the seasoning, and stir in the cream or yogurt. Divide the cutlets or steaks among 4 serving plates, and pour over the sauce, garnishing with a sprinkling of extra fresh herbs that you've just cut from your window box – or bought in the local supermarket!

Mustard loin of wild boar

Serves 2

2 tablespoons olive oil

2 wild boar loin steaks, about 175g (6oz) each

1 teaspoon wholegrain mustard

100ml (3½fl oz) chicken stock

2 tablespoons crème fraîche

juice of 1 lemon

a few sprigs of fresh flat-leaf parsley, leaves picked

Also good with
chicken breast fillet

The loin is a particularly tender part of the boar, and as such can be cooked quickly without coming to any harm. This recipe is exceptionally easy and fast, and the mustard really complements the wild boar.

1 Heat a non-stick or heavy frying pan until hot, and add the olive oil. Sear the loin steaks on each side for 5 minutes, then remove to a plate.

2 Add the mustard and chicken stock to the pan, and bring to a simmer, whisking in the crème fraîche.

3 Return the wild boar steaks to the pan, and add the lemon juice and parsley. Cook for a further 8–10 minutes, keeping an eye on the steaks so that they don't dry out. Serve hot.

Zebra

The name 'zebra' is believed to originate from an old Portuguese word meaning 'wild ass', and the zebra does indeed belong to the genus *Equus* and is therefore is a relative of the horse and donkey – although it has not ever been truly domesticated. Two species of zebra have become endangered: Grevy's zebra, through overhunting for its skins, and the mountain zebra, whose habitat has been all but destroyed. The plains zebra population is much more plentiful and carefully managed, and the animals can only be sourced as part of CITES (Convention on International Trade in Endangered Species of Wild Fauna and Flora). Amazingly, the beautiful patterns on each coat are unique to individual animals, and the zebra foals are born brown and white, not black and white.

ORIGINS
Member of the equid family made up of three species and found across eastern and southern Africa; only the plains zebra is harvested for its meat.

COMMON CUTS
Similar to antelope in terms of structure. Hence we recommend fillet, loin and haunch for steaks, and roasting joints.

TASTES LIKE
So pure and light that it tastes of grass, the meat is light red in colour, with a texture like beef rather than venison.

BEST WAYS TO COOK
Best cooked only to medium-rare. The fillet steaks are glorious when pan-fried to a crisp on the outside and left rare on the inside.

SIGNATURE DISH
Zebra teriyaki (see pages 168–9).

Zebra teriyaki

Serves 2

2 zebra fillet steaks, about
150g (5oz) each
a little olive oil
2 tablespoons sake or
dry sherry
2 tablespoons Japanese or
dark soy sauce
2 tablespoons sweet sherry
1 teaspoon sugar

Also good with
duck breasts

Incredibly quick to prepare, this is fast food at its best. Serve with a salad that you have prepared ahead of time or, if you choose vegetables as your accompaniment, make sure that you have them ready to go. Your steaks will take only 10–12 minutes in total to cook. Be warned: you need to have smoking-hot oil and a good strong pan in which to sizzle the sauce.

1 Take the steaks out of the refrigerator at least an hour ahead of cooking time; they should be at room temperature by the time you use them.

2 Place a heavy frying pan over a high heat, and cover the bottom with a film of olive oil. When the oil is smoking hot, add the steaks to the pan, and sear for 6–8 minutes, turning once during the cooking time.

3 Once the steaks are seared on both sides, spoon over the sake or dry sherry. Cover the pan, and leave to sizzle for 2–3 minutes while the sake or sherry does its work. Transfer the zebra steaks to a warm plate, and leave to rest while you make the teriyaki sauce.

4 Add the soy sauce, sweet sherry and sugar to the pan, and stir with a wooden spoon, scraping up any bits stuck to the bottom of the pan. Bring the sauce to the boil, and reduce in volume by about half. Return the steaks and any accumulated juices to the pan, and quickly swirl around in the sauce until piping hot and ready to serve.

Zebra carpaccio with chocolate vinaigrette

Serves 2

200–225g (7–8oz) zebra fillet
or loin, thinly sliced

Chocolate vinaigrette
30g (1oz) dark chocolate (at
least 70% cocoa solids)
juice of ½ lemon
2 tablespoons olive oil
pinch of dried red chilli flakes
1 teaspoon Dijon mustard
1 teaspoon caster sugar
1 teaspoon balsamic vinegar
1 teaspoon white wine vinegar
1 tablespoon chopped chives

Also good with
venison

Zebra and chocolate – who would have thought that they would make such a lovely combination, their flavours melding in a divine culinary alchemy. In fact, the concept of mixing chocolate with game meats is now old hat, but we think that we've been at least a little bit on the adventurous side by using zebra. It has to be zebra fillet or loin, though, not haunch, as the tenderest meat should be used to make carpaccio.

1 For the carpaccio, take each slice of zebra, and sandwich between two sheets of cling film. Pound with a meat mallet or the side of a rolling pin until paper-thin and evenly flattened. Arrange all the slices in a single layer on a plate, and leave to chill for 10 minutes.

2 Meanwhile, make the vinaigrette. Melt the chocolate in a bowl set over a pan of simmering water, then allow to cool slightly. In a small bowl, whisk together all the vinaigrette ingredients until well combined.

3 When ready to serve, drizzle the dressing over the carpaccio, and serve immediately.

Stir-fry of zebra with horseradish

Serves 2

1 tablespoon sunflower oil

250g (9oz) zebra fillet, cut into thin strips

$\frac{1}{2}$ red onion, finely sliced

100g (3$\frac{1}{2}$oz) Savoy cabbage, thinly sliced

2 carrots, cut diagonally into slices 5mm ($\frac{1}{4}$in) thick

150g (5oz) cooked baby new potatoes, cut into chunks

75ml (2$\frac{1}{2}$fl oz) beef stock

2 tablespoons horseradish sauce

sea salt and freshly ground black pepper

Also good with
strips of beef fillet

When we tried this dish out on my family (Jeannie's), it was a testament to their upbringing that, when we said that this was a stir-fry with a difference, my daughter Bryony replied: 'Hmmm, yes, I've never seen potatoes used in a stir-fry before.' My children have, of course, been used as 'guinea pigs' on many occasions throughout their teenage years, eating a wide variety of meats and testing out many of the recipes included in this book. Bless them. Never a word of complaint!

1 Heat a large wok until very hot, then add the oil. Add the zebra strips, and quickly stir-fry for 5 minutes until browned, but still rare inside. Remove from the wok with a slotted spoon, and set aside to rest on a warm plate.

2 Now add the onion to the wok, and stir-fry for 1 minute. Tip in the Savoy cabbage and carrots, and stir-fry for 2 minutes. Add the potatoes and beef stock, and bring to the boil. Reduce the heat slightly, and simmer for 1–2 minutes until the potatoes are heated through.

3 Stir in the horseradish sauce, then return the zebra and any accumulated juices to the wok. Season to taste with salt and black pepper, quickly toss through and serve immediately.

Zebra with red wine and shallot marmalade

Serves 4

2 tablespoons black peppercorns, quite coarsely ground

2 tablespoons pink peppercorns, quite coarsely ground

1 tablespoon sea salt

4 zebra steaks, about 225g (8oz) each

For the red wine and shallot marmalade

2 tablespoons butter

2 tablespoons extra virgin olive oil

1 tablespoon soft brown sugar

225g (8oz) shallots, finely sliced

500ml (16fl oz) red wine

1 tablespoon chopped thyme leaves

sea salt and freshly ground black pepper

Also good with
lamb steaks

We suggest that you always undercook these steaks, and leave to rest before serving, as zebra meat has a flavour of its own that needs to develop and is best experienced at the pink (medium-rare) stage for the more delicate among us. As far as we are concerned, the steaks should be singed dark on the outside and remain blue on the inside.

1 Mix together the ground peppercorns and salt in a small bowl. Lay the zebra steaks on a wooden chopping board, and use the peppercorn mixture to coat the zebra steaks liberally on both sides, pressing the steaks down onto the board so that the coating sticks firmly. Set aside.

2 To make the marmalade, melt the butter with the oil and sugar in a heavy saucepan over a medium-high heat. When the sugar has dissolved, add the shallots and cook gently over a medium heat for 10 minutes until caramelised. Pour in the wine, reduce the heat slightly and simmer until the liquid has reduced to a quarter of its original amount. Remove from the heat, sprinkle in the thyme and season with salt and black pepper. Set aside in a warm place until needed.

3 Heat a grill or charcoal barbecue until the flames have died away and the coals are glowing-hot. Sear the steaks on both sides until cooked to your liking – medium-rare at most is best. Remove to a plate, and leave to rest for a few minutes to allow the meat to relax and the flavours to develop.

4 To serve, top each of the steaks with a spoonful of the shallot marmalade. (You can serve the marmalade hot, warm or at room temperature.) This would be perfect served with thick slices of oven-roasted sweet potato.

Zebra saltimbocca

Serves 2 as canapés
or starter

2 zebra rump or fillet steaks,
about 170g (6oz) each

4 slices Parma ham

4 slices haloumi or
mozzarella cheese

2 small fresh sage leaves

1 tablespoon olive oil

sea salt and freshly ground
black pepper

Traditionally, saltimbocca is made with thinly sliced veal escalopes, but we have chosen to use zebra steaks instead, which give extra flavour without being overpowering. The most fitting description I have ever given for this meat came spontaneously when I first tasted zebra at a South African restaurant in London. It truly tasted of grass, so fresh and different were the flavours that I experienced.

1 Preheat the oven to 200°C/400°F/Gas Mark 6.

2 Lay the steaks on a large chopping board lined with a large sheet of cling film. Fold the cling film over the top of the steaks, and pound with a meat mallet or the side of a rolling pin until evenly flattened – they should be about 2cm (¾in) thick. Season on both sides with salt and black pepper (don't forget to remove the cling film). Arrange 2 slices of ham and 2 slices of cheese on top of each zebra escalope, with 2 sage leaves on top, then roll up. Secure with kitchen string or cocktail sticks. Brush each roll with the oil.

3 Heat a large non-stick ovenproof frying pan (cast-iron is great) until smoking. Add the zebra escalopes, and cook for 6–8 minutes, turning occasionally, until browned on all sides. Reduce the temperature if the steaks are cooking too quickly.

4 Transfer the pan to the oven and, if you don't like your meat too rare, cook for a further 6–8 minutes, turning once. Remove from the oven, carefully remove the cocktails sticks (if using) and leave to rest for 2–3 minutes. Slice into thin rounds, arrange on a bed of watercress and rocket, and serve as canapés or an impressive starter.

Index

ACKNOWLEDGMENTS

We would like to say a grateful thank
you to Scott Pack and all his team,
without whom this book would simply
not exist – for their kindness, endless
patience and professionalism in guiding
us through the whole process.

Jeannie – I would like to pay tribute to
my beautiful children, Bryony, John, and
Dave, for putting up with all the cooking
experiments and for their enthusiasm,
love and unstinting support in all that I
do. To my mum and dad, who have had
to put up with my crazy adventures all
these years; to my wonderful partner,
Ben, and his little girl, Jessica, who have
been prepared to be guinea pigs and
eat the strangest of foods on many,
many occasions; and to my wonderful
fellow musketeers Josie and Steph, who
are just always there for me.

Rachel – I would like to thank my lovely
Shirley for having never-ending faith in
everything I do, for always being there
for me and for all her loving support.
Love and thanks to my parents – Pops
for teaching me the brick principle and
Mum for the strength and love you have
always surrounded me with. A huge
thank you to all my wonderful friends
dotted around the globe – you know
who you are. To you all, you have made
me into the person I am today, making
me thankful that you are in my life.

The girls want also to express a big
thank you to Diane, for being the
backbone of the business while they 'go
gadding', and to Squeak, for buying Ted
and Shemane Nugent's Kill It and Grill
It, and sparking off the whole idea.